BMW MINI

JAMES TAYLOR

AMBERLEY

First published 2022

Amberley Publishing
The Hill, Stroud,
Gloucestershire, GL5 4EP

www.amberley-books.com

ISBN: 978 1 3981 0981 0 (print)
ISBN: 978 1 3981 0982 7 (ebook)

British Library Cataloguing in Publication Data.
A catalogue record for this book is available from the British Library.

Typeset in 10pt on 13pt Celeste.
Typesetting by SJmagic DESIGN SERVICES, India.
Printed in the UK.

Contents

1

In the Beginning

Somehow, British Leyland never got around to replacing the original Mini. The model that had represented a revolution in small-car design had been such a strong seller when its makers became part of that larger corporation in 1968 that there had been no rush to develop a model that could take over from it. Besides, there were very many higher priorities for the newly formed company, and that would remain the case for more than another three decades.

Not that the company did not try. There were in fact several attempts to design a new Mini. The man who had designed the original car that was launched in 1959 was

It might have been a MINI, but it was a lot bigger than the original Mini! (Pixabay)

Alec Issigonis, and even though he had been moved sideways after British Leyland was formed, he still believed he had some valid ideas. In 1967, he had stepped down from his job as head of new car development at BMC to concentrate on the Mini 9X, and he continued to work on this for many more years.

The 9X was never approved for production, but by 1972 British Leyland were stung into action by the number of new small cars beginning to appear from rival makers – many of them drawing on the design advances made by the original Mini well over a decade earlier. Designers began to look seriously at a new 'supermini' that was known internally as the ADO74 project. As insurance, work also began on a second car, closer in size to the original Mini, and this eventually became ADO88.

Somehow ADO88 survived the multiple reorganisations within British Leyland in the 1970s, and was ready for production when Michael Edwardes was appointed as the corporation's new top man in 1977. However, Edwardes was disappointed by reactions to the car at customer research clinics, realised it was not going to be the big success that the company needed so badly, and halted production plans. ADO88 then evolved into LC8, the supermini that was released as the MiniMetro in 1980. By this stage, British Leyland was desperately short of cash, and the MiniMetro (later known simply as the Metro) was seen as its major chance of survival.

Fortunately, the Metro went onto be a success, but in the meantime the idea of a direct replacement for the original Mini had been lost. There was no money to fund such a car, and as the original model was still selling strongly – if not quite as strongly as it once had – it was easy enough for British Leyland management to defer the question of its replacement. The question was still unresolved when a slimmed-down British Leyland was renamed as the Rover Group in 1986.

Plant Oxford, as it is known, had once been the BMC factory at Cowley, near Oxford. (Lobster 1/ WikiMedia Commons)

BMW also established a dedicated pressings plant at Swindon to supply the assembly lines at Cowley. (DeFacto/WikiMedia Commons)

So the original Mini was long overdue for retirement by the time the Rover Group established a serious project to replace it. The first moves were made in 1993, when Design Director Gordon Sked asked his team to sketch up ideas. Sked's vision was ambitious. His designers were not to feel constrained by any need for carry-over engineering, but they were to try to capture the innovative spirit of the 1959 original.

Two concepts by designer Oliver Le Grice were turned into full-size models. One was simply referred to as the Mini and had a similar footprint to the existing car, gaining interior space through extra height. The other was a long-wheelbase version that was known as the Midi. These were the front runners for the new Mini by January 1994, when the Rover Group was somewhat abruptly sold to the German carmaker BMW.

The Germans were already well aware of the immense goodwill associated with the Mini brand and were very keen indeed to ensure that it was not squandered. As a result, they took a keen interest in the project to replace it. From the start, however, they took a very different approach from the British designers. They envisaged a new Mini as an evolution of the old one, and they believed that the correct solution was to develop a small car that was a visually recognisable descendant of the original but would incorporate modern technology. They wanted to build on what the Mini brand stood for, and in particular to exploit the sporting legacy of the Mini Cooper.

BMW owned the Rover Group, and so BMW got their way. A key early appointment was Frank Stephenson, an Anglo-American designer already on the BMW staff who was now put in charge of the overall appearance of the new Mini. In early 1995, proposals were invited from the Rover designers at Canley, BMW DesignWorks in Los Angeles, Stephenson's team in Munich, and the Giugiaro studio in Italy.

Several of these proposals were developed further during 1995, and a design competition was held that October. A committee of seven BMW executives and seven Rover executives reviewed all the proposals, among them the 1993 Mini and Midi concepts, and unanimously voted for the one from Frank Stephenson's team. It certainly ticked all the boxes, encapsulating the cheeky and friendly appearance of the original Mini with its wheel-at-each-corner stance and at the same time updating it within the slightly larger dimensions needed to meet modern safety requirements. Wheel arch extensions in contrasting black blended into the underbody sills and deliberately recalled the arches added to later versions of the original Mini to cover their widened tracks.

The clay model was digitised in Munich and the data was sent to Rover's Gaydon headquarters, where the British designers were asked to prepare the design for production. However, they appear not to have given up without a fight. When Stephenson visited the Gaydon studios to check on progress, he discovered that Rover had modified his design. As he told *Classic Car Weekly* (5 May 2021), 'I was aghast. My mission was to take my theme into production, and now I felt very much like a cowboy in Indian territory.' The Rover

BMW promotion and marketing of the MINI would always be important factors in its success. This car was displayed for a time at the BMW Museum in Munich, Germany. (Jiří Sedláček/WikiMedia Commons)

team held their ground until 1996, when BMW's Wolfgang Reitzle, who had been put in to oversee Rover Group on the German company's behalf, put his foot down and insisted that Rover should accept the design as it was.

So it was that the new car took shape to Stephenson's design during 1997, and a series of customer clinics that year demonstrated that BMW had been right to insist. Strong scores in the clinics 'helped the Rover guys understand that we had a hit on our hands,' said Stephenson.

Meanwhile, the engineering teams at Rover were developing the hardware for the new car to meet BMW specifications. The project had been allocated the R50 code name during 1995, using a BMW numbering system with the R standing for Rover. The project started well, but soon descended into a rivalry between the British and German engineers allocated to it as the two groups repeatedly fell out over suspension and packaging issues. It was not the happiest of times for anyone involved, but the new Mini's suspension was settled as combining space-saving MacPherson struts at the front with BMW's acclaimed coil-sprung 'Z-axle' at the rear, and the end result was an excellent piece of engineering.

There were disagreements over the choice of a manual gearbox, too. BMW had wanted to award the contract to its own favoured supplier, Getrag, but the choice fell on the R65 or Midland gearbox that was being made by Rover. (The R65 name had been chosen by Rover and had nothing to do with the similar BMW codes used for Rover car designs.) BMW wanted an automatic option, too, and was content with the choice of a CVT type similar to the one already available in some Rover models and made in Germany by ZF.

Engines became a further bone of contention. The Rover engineers favoured their own K-series four-cylinders, which were already in production and had a modern design of which they were very proud. However, BMW did not share their enthusiasm, but instead focused on creating a brand-new engine through an international joint venture with Chrysler in the USA. Chrysler needed small engines for its European cars, and in 1997 the two companies formed Tritec to design and build engines for both of them.

Low manufacturing costs were a key aim for both parties. To that end a decision was made to locate the new engine factory in Brazil, at Campo Largo near Curituba in the south of the country. The Tritec name reflected the involvement of the three nations of Germany (BMW), Britain (Rover) and the USA (Chrysler), but the new engine was never intended only to go into Rover and Chrysler products. To increase production volumes and so drive down costs, it was to be offered to other car makers, and in due course two Chinese car makers – Chery and Lifan – would become major customers. The factory was built to produce up to 400,000 engines a year, but in practice it only ever achieved about half that.

Design work began immediately, and the new Tritec engine embraced the latest technology. It was drawn up as a four-cylinder design for transverse installation, with enough flexibility to provide sizes of between 1.4 and 1.6 litres. There would be a sixteen-valve configuration for maximum efficiency, but for cost reasons there would be only a single overhead camshaft and the block would be made of cast iron. The head, of course, would be aluminium.

BMW was in no doubt that a massive public relations and marketing effort would be needed to ensure the success of the new Mini, not least because of the worldwide affection felt for the old one. So the programme began in 1997, two years before the planned 1999 launch of the new car. At the Geneva Motor Show that March, the Mini and Midi concepts

The engine of the first MINI models was a product of the Tritec joint-venture company in Brazil.

were displayed under the names of Mini Spiritual and Mini Spiritual Too in order to reassure the world that work was going ahead on a new Mini. The world duly took note but did not rush to acclaim the two models. BMW in turn took note, no doubt pleased that its decision not to base the new model on these concepts had been vindicated.

As a second stage in the public relations game, another rejected Mini concept was shown in public at that year's Monte Carlo Rally. This was a most attractive running prototype that was built on an MGF floorpan, with mid-engine and rear-wheel drive. Known as the ACV30, it had originated with BMW's Dreamworks studio in California. The name stood for Anniversary Concept Vehicle, and the 30 reflected the thirty years between its construction and the original Mini's 1964 Monte Carlo Rally win.

The design was supposedly a collaboration between BMW's Adriaan van Hooydonk and Frank Stephenson, and it incorporated two features that anticipated Stephenson's production design for the new Mini – large wheel arches and a 'floating' roof in a

The Rover Group envisaged the new Mini as revolutionary rather than evolutionary. These two concepts, Mini and long-wheelbase Midi, date from 1993 and were revived by BMW as 'teases' in 1997 under the names of Spiritual and Spiritual Too.

BMW always wanted an evolutionary design, and this was the ACV30 – Anniversary Concept Vehicle – pictured with a Mini-Cooper rally car from 1967. The concept had a much more obvious appeal than Rover's efforts.

contrasting colour. Its attractive interior design by BMW's Ivan Lampkin also anticipated the eventual production design, with a prominent centrally mounted speedometer (like that of the original Mini) but more bare metal than BMW was prepared to countenance. It was a step closer to the real thing.

The real thing – or, more accurately, an approximation of it – was then displayed at a joint BMW and Rover press conference at the Frankfurt Motor Show in October 1997. The press were told of the plans to use the Tritec engine, and that three different models were planned. They were not expecting to see a real car, which was driven onto a stage and then, fairly quickly, off again. This running prototype had the body shape chosen for production, and it was a convincing visual representation of the car that would become the new Mini Cooper. In reality, it was not a full prototype but rather a 'mule', with the planned body mounted on the platform and running gear of a Fiat Punto, which just happened to be the right size!

Rover officials at the show confirmed that this was indeed to be the new Mini, and John Cooper (of Formula 1 and Mini Cooper fame) was on hand to tell BBC TV News that 'It's a Mini and it's going to be the new Mini. It's got a wheel in each corner, it looks like a Mini. I know it's a little bigger and it's had to be modified slightly for the safety regulations and that sort of thing, but I think the team at Rovers have done a wonderful job on it, actually,

Tease time again, but this time the picture released to the press showed the design chosen for production. In fact, this was the 'mule' car, built on a Fiat Punto platform.

The Mini Cooper with its sporting heritage was always central to the BMW marketing plan, and the 'tease' car was dressed with Mini Cooper badges.

and I'm very proud and I'm sure Issigonis in the 21st century would have been very proud of it if he had seen it.'

There were some very positive reactions to the appearance of this car, which had the desired effect of raising public anticipation of the new Mini. Behind the scenes, however, all was not well, either with relations between Rover and BMW or with the new Mini itself. In particular, by autumn 1998 the prototypes were demonstrating that it was not going to be easy to build cars to the target weight. The extra weight had an adverse effect on the crisp handling that was needed. Worse, the early engines coming from the Tritec plant in Brazil were not meeting their power targets or their driveability criteria. For some time, these were critical issues. The target of a 1999 launch date was clearly not going to be met.

Worse still was what was happening within BMW in Germany. There had for a long time been two factions within the company, one supporting Chairman Bernd Pischetsrieder's belief in the Rover Group, and the other supporting Wolfgang Reitzle's view that the Rover Cars side of the business was beyond saving and should be sold off or closed down. Even Pischetsrieder was under no illusions about Rover Cars' disappointing performance, and he said so, painfully and publicly, in 1998: 'We have made good progress with Rover, but it is not enough.' BMW told the British government that they might have to close the Longbridge factory where they planned to build the new Mini unless there was a turnaround in Rover's profitability – or unless the government provided £200 million in financial support. The German newspapers began to refer to Rover as 'the English patient', using the title of a contemporary cinema success.

There was only one way this could end, and the disagreement was finally resolved at a board meeting on 5 February 1999 in Munich. First Pischetsrieder and then Reitzle resigned their posts. The board ultimately resolved to dispose of the Rover Group.

That decision meant that the company would also be disposing of its two flagship projects for Rover: the new third-generation Range Rover and the new Mini. Ultimately, the Range Rover did go to another company, when Ford bought the Land Rover business in summer 2000 and BMW agreed to finish the engineering needed to put it into production in late 2001. On the Mini, however, BMW dug its collective heels in. The board resolved to sell off Rover Cars as a business but to retain the Mini project, and to retain the Rover share of the joint engine project with Chrysler in Brazil.

It is not hard to see the reasoning here, or to understand the pride that the Germans took in the car into which they had invested so much time and effort. Just a year earlier,

Bodyshell assembly at the MINI plant in Oxford during 2001. (BMW Press)

An early MINI bodyshell receives its base coats in the paint shop. (BMW Press)

This 2001 picture of the production lines at Plant Oxford shows the 'marriage' of the MINI bodyshell with its rear suspension. (BMW Press)

Here, the power unit – an early Tritecc engine – is about to be fitted to the MINI bodyshell. (BMW Press)

the company had been able to expand its market reach upwards with the acquisition of the Rolls-Royce brand. With the new Mini, it planned to expand its range downwards without harming the image of the core BMW brand. Besides, there were plans to make the new Mini available in countries where the Mini brand had not previously been sold, notably the potentially enormously lucrative USA. It was simply too good an opportunity to miss.

Rover designer Geoff Upex remembered that a truck arrived at the Gaydon studio on the very day that BMW signed the contract to sell Rover and that everything relating to the new Mini was loaded in it and taken away to Munich. Work at Longbridge to prepare the Rover plant for manufacture of the new car was suspended. BMW quickly decided to sell Longbridge with the Rover Cars business – indeed, it would have been unsaleable without its primary assembly plant – and to relocate Mini production to the Cowley plant near Oxford.

All this, and the sale of the Rover and Land Rover businesses, took time. While Land Rover went to a jubilant Ford, the rump of the Rover Cars business, which included the MG sports car brand, was sold to a group of businessmen called the Phoenix Consortium. It emerged as MG Rover. By the time BMW was able to focus fully on its plans for the new Mini, it was clear that production could not begin in earnest until early 2001, which was two years after the date originally planned.

Branding was vital, and this was the emblem designed for the new Mini, this time with capital letters – MINI. (Pixabay)

An early MINI Cooper retained at the Oxford factory stands behind a 2021 model on the end of the assembly line. The picture was taken to celebrate twenty years of production. (BMW Press)

Nevertheless, BMW made good use of the extra time it now had. The problems of excess weight and underperforming engines could be resolved. The new Mini no longer needed to be tied into product plans for other models from the Rover Group. It could instead take on a trajectory of its own. BMW drew up plans to make the Mini into a standalone brand, which would draw its image from the heritage of the original Mini but would be distinctive. To that end, there was a subtle but important rebranding exercise, as Mini became MINI with capital letters.

Four years between the public 'tease' of the chosen production shape and its appearance in the showrooms was too long. So BMW kept public interest high through some slick public relations work. At the Mini '40th Birthday Party' event at Silverstone in August 1999, they displayed a full prototype as a show of confidence. At the Paris Motor Show that opened on 30 September 2000, they showed two more production-ready Mini prototypes, each one fully representative of the eventual production models except for their colours of Candy Blue and Flamenco Orange, neither of which has ever appeared on a production car. The show stand also displayed some 'tease' illustrations of possible future models, including a convertible and a pick-up truck.

At the Frankfurt Show a year later, the concept theme was continued with a hydrogen-powered MINI that was an extension of BMW's long-term experiments with hydrogen as a fuel for the internal combustion engine. It was an interesting way of adding excitement to the MINI display, because by then the real thing had already gone on sale.

2

The First Generation, 2001–2006

BMW envisaged the MINI as a major brand in its own right that would have an appeal far beyond that of the original Mini. Clever marketing was going to be the key to this, but the plan was always to begin with a relatively small range of models and then expand as quickly as market acceptance allowed.

So when production began at the Oxford plant in April 2001, there were just two basic models. These were the entry-level MINI One and the more expensive and performance-oriented MINI Cooper. Both were known internally as R50 types, and each had a different version of the same 1.6-litre Tritec engine. Nevertheless, there was also a 1.4-litre engine for Greece and Portugal, where taxation would otherwise hinder sales. Both models came with the choice of a manual or a CVT automatic gearbox, and sales began in the UK in July.

Range expansion began in 2002 with the supercharged Cooper S. This was the R53 type and was readily distinguishable by its bonnet scoop and twin exhausts emerging in the

The dashboard design was heavily inspired by that of the original Mini, with its large centrally mounted speedometer. Even though the MINI was built in Britain, BMW focused on European markets and issued many press pictures showing left-hand-drive models.

centre of the rear valance. Production volumes increased, too, not least as exports of Cooper and Cooper S models to the USA began in March 2002.

Next, BMW increased the MINI's appeal to economy-minded buyers in 2003 with a diesel engine option, initially available only in the entry-level MINI One. So by the time the whole range was given a mild facelift in July 2004 – three years into production – there were three models (One, Cooper and Cooper S) and four engines (1.6 petrol in two states of tune, 1.6 supercharged petrol, and diesel). All these models shared the same three-door body style, called the Hatch in Britain but the Hardtop in the USA. The next expansion of the range brought a second body style, the R52 Convertible. This was made available in One, Cooper and Cooper S guises.

These were the models that remained in production until a more extensively revised second-generation MINI arrived in November 2006. Missing from the range of R50 (One and Cooper), R52 (Convertible) and R53 (Cooper S) types was an R51 model. Plans for this, a long-wheelbase model, did not go beyond the concept stage.

MINI One

At the 1997 press presentation in Frankfurt, BMW had suggested that the entry-level model would be called the Mini Minor, a name used for the 1959 Morris version of the original car. However, the name Minor was hardly appropriate for a car that was intended to stand out in a crowd, and by the time production began in spring 2001 the name had become MINI One.

The MINI One was easy to recognise thanks to its black grille. However, options abounded, and this early car has non-standard wheels from the large options list.

As the least expensive model in the new MINI range, this version lacked much of the equipment that came on its more expensive siblings. Nevertheless, central to the MINI marketing plan was a vast options list, with everything from air conditioning and satellite navigation to leather upholstery and alternative alloy wheel designs. BMW knew that customers enjoyed dialling their own personal requirements into the specification of their cars, and the MINI brand would go on to exploit that to the hilt.

The One carried appropriate badging on its hatchback and had a rather cheeky-looking reversing light mounted in the centre of the rear apron. The wheels had a 15-inch size unless one of the larger options was ordered. Characteristic of these cars were a black-painted radiator grille and a concealed exhaust tailpipe, while the roof was (again, unless to order) painted the same colour as the body.

The standard MINI One came with the 1.6-litre (1,598-cc) Tritec four-cylinder petrol engine, mounted transversely and driving the front wheels. With 90PS and 140Nm (104 lb ft) of torque, this gave the car a top speed of 112 mph and acceleration from 0–60 mph of 10.6 seconds. The 1.4-litre version of the same engine for export had 75PS and the same torque. Performance was correspondingly reduced, but of course the MINI's cheeky good looks, personalised specification, and go-kart handling were still part of the package.

The standard gearbox was of course the five-speed manual R65 type made by Rover, which boasted a very slick change and well-chosen ratios. However, an item added to that vast extra-cost options list in 2002 was an automatic gearbox that gave easier driving with almost as much zest. Nominally a six-speed gearbox, it was in fact a CVT (Continuously Variable Transmission) type manufactured in Germany by ZF as their VT1F type. This gearbox would remain available until the end of first-generation MINI production, but the manual gearbox would be changed when the range was facelifted in summer 2004.

Cooper

The MINI Cooper was central to the range in more ways than one. Not only was it the mid-range model but it also encapsulated the spirit of the original sporting Mini, also called Cooper. This had been introduced in 1961 as a 'performance' version of the original car, and benefited from an engine tuned by racing-car constructor John Cooper, who allowed his name to be used on the cars in return for a royalty on each one that was sold.

Cooper models of the new MINI came with an engine that delivered an appropriate amount of extra performance: a headline 125 mph top speed and a 0–60 mph time of 9.3 seconds. Power was quoted as 116PS and torque as 149Nm (110 lb ft). Yet this engine was not as different from the power unit of the MINI One as those figures might suggest. The Cooper actually had the same 1.6-litre Tritec four-cylinder with a different management 'chip' to deliver the extra power and torque. And – whisper it – it was this version of the engine that would also be used in several Chrysler cars and also in some cars built in China for domestic consumption.

Chrome bumpers and grille bars mark this car out as an early MINI Cooper, although the buyer chose to have a body-coloured roof instead of a contrasting colour. (Thomas Doerfer/Wikimedia Commons)

Coopers had to look different, of course. All of them came with the roof painted in white or black to contrast with the body, and with mirror bodies painted to match it. They had a bright radiator grille, different wheels, a discreet 'Cooper' badge on the tail, and a single exhaust peeping out from below the rear valance. Standard equipment levels were generally higher than those on the MINI One, and yet there was still plenty on the options list to tempt a Cooper buyer.

Cooper S

The top-model MINI was held over until 2002 and once again carried an established name from the original Mini. The Cooper S was cosmetically much like the mid-range Cooper, but there were some subtle differences. At the front was a very visible air-intake slot just above the radiator grille. At the rear was a stylish spoiler above the back window, with the third brake light in its centre. The bumper valance had extra air vents, twin exhaust pipes emerged under the centre of that valance, and of course there were Cooper S badges.

Another chrome bumper, a prominent Cooper badge, and a single exhaust pipe were all hallmarks of the Cooper models. (Thomas Doerfer/Wikimedia Commons)

The fuel filler cap had a bright finish, and, of course, there were special wheels and several special touches in the passenger cabin.

That extra air intake in the bonnet – usually called a 'scoop' – had a genuinely practical purpose, which was to feed air to the intercooler associated with the supercharger that gave the Cooper S its extra performance. The supercharger was an Eaton M45 type, neatly packaged with the engine, and with a lower compression ratio than the standard Cooper (to guard against misfiring) the Cooper S engine produced an impressive 160PS and 220Nm (163 lb ft) of torque. That translated into a top speed of 133 mph and a 0–60 mph time of just 7 seconds. 'Not the fastest hot hatch,' said *Autocar*, 'just the most entertaining.'

It was not only the customers who were impressed. An international jury of experts gave this engine first prize in its size category in the International Engine of the Year awards for 2003, and the same year it won the top place among Ward's 10 Best Engines. Much less publicised than this, of course, was that the Cooper S had gearboxes that were different from the other MINIs. The R65 manual gearbox was not strong enough to take the torque of the supercharged engine, and BMW replaced it by a six-speed Getrag G285 type (its top gear being an overdrive). For good measure, they also used a conventional six-speed automatic made by Aisin instead of the CVT type in other MINIs.

Attractive two-tone interiors were standard on the more expensive models.

Diesel

No diesel engine had ever been available for the original Mini, but times had changed. Diesel power was popular in Europe, particularly in France and Italy, and BMW knew that it had to offer a diesel option. Developing a dedicated small diesel engine was a cost too far at this stage, and so the company resolved to buy one in. The obvious candidates available from PSA Peugeot-Citroen and Renault were too big to fit the engine bay, but after an eighteenth-month search they found one that would do the job in the shape of Toyota's 1ND-TV type.

Toyota had designed this single-overhead-camshaft engine for low emissions and fuel consumption, low noise levels, and low weight. An aluminium cylinder block gave it a total weight of just 99 kg, and a variable-geometry turbocharger gave it a smooth and punchy power delivery. Toyota introduced it to Europe during 2002 in their Yaris models, with the same 1,364-cc capacity that BMW would use. In BMW form, it came with a dual-mass flywheel and slightly more torque than the Yaris had; the peak was 180Nm (133 lb ft) at 2,000 rpm, while the 74PS maximum power was generated at 4,000 rpm.

Power, then, was fractionally below that of the 1.4-litre Tritec petrol engine, but the torque was much more substantial and gave quite spirited acceleration; 0–60 mph took 13.8 seconds. With the six-speed manual gearbox from the Cooper S, the diesel engine gave a little under 60mpg in a MINI One. The combination was persuasive. It became even more persuasive when these outputs were raised in November 2005 to 89PS and 190Nm (140 lb ft) at the same engine speeds, and the top speed went up to 109 mph.

Convertible

The original Mini had been on sale for thirty-three years before a convertible version became available through the showrooms in 1992. Never a huge seller, it nevertheless made clear that there was a market for a convertible MINI – and besides, other makers of cars in the same class such as Volkswagen and Peugeot were already offering such an option.

So a Convertible MINI was designed, taking the model code R52. It was previewed at the Geneva Show in March 2004 and went on sale later that year to an enthusiastic reception. In 2005, claimed the MINI Press Office, the Convertible outsold its nearest rival by a huge 27 per cent. This was success indeed.

A key element in the model's success was obviously fun; this was a small and cheeky car that could be thrown about with a fair amount of abandon, and the addition of a top that could be lowered in good weather was bound to meet approval. But other factors were at work, too, and among them were ease of use and good looks. An electro-hydraulic roof

The air scoop was the dominant recognition feature of a Cooper S. Here it is, pictured on an early R52 Convertible model.

The twin tailpipes would indicate a Cooper S even if the badge was not visible. The Convertible hood was quite bulky when lowered, but the fun quotient was high!

The Convertible top fitted neatly when erected. This dark-coloured Cooper S registered in Germany shows how smart the R52 could look. (M 93/WikiMedia Commons)

The boot opening was restricted on the Convertible MINI, but the Easy Load option opened it up a little more at the top to improve access.

mechanism opened the top fully at the touch of a button, or would open the front section by just 40 cm (15.7 inches) to allow a comfortable through-flow of air – much in the style of a 1930s 'three-position' drophead coupé. The soft top did fold down into a rather large mass that restricted rearward vision, but when erected it formed a very neat shape that was entirely in keeping with the basic MINI profile.

The R52 Convertible could not, of course, have a hatchback like the parent R50 model. Instead, it had a drop-down boot lid with external hinges that very much recalled the original Mini. The boot itself was really was rather small, especially when the soft top was folded down into it, but an ingenious Easy Load System did allow maximum use of the space available.

The R52 MINI Convertible found ready acceptance, and actually stayed in production for nearly three years after the other first-generation MINI models had been replaced. Its popularity granted BMW valuable extra time to develop its second-generation successor.

The Facelift

BMW policy was to facelift models just after the mid-point of their intended production life, and no exception was made for the MINI. Nevertheless, there was no point in changing a winning formula, and so the changes that were made in summer 2004 were not apparent from a quick glance.

The mid-2004 facelift is seen here on a Cooper. The picture shows the additional chrome elements at the front and the revised lighting arrangements.

There were changes at the rear for 2004, too, but the Cooper retained its distinctive badge and single tailpipe.

Completely invisible was a new manual gearbox. Perhaps sensing the imminent demise of Rover (which actually collapsed in 2005), BMW switched to its favoured supplier Getrag in Germany, and that company's 52BG five-speed type replaced the Rover R65. It was just as slick as the transmission it replaced.

All models, including the Convertible that was introduced at the time of the facelift, had some minor changes to the headlights. There were also new front and rear bumpers for base and Cooper models, but the Cooper S kept its original design. If these changes were not very obvious, it was easy to tell one of the newer cars from the rear, where the reversing light had disappeared from the centre of the bumper to be replaced by a pair of lights incorporated in the main clusters.

The facelift was a little more obvious inside the passenger cabin, where a three-spoke steering wheel replaced the original two spoke design. The rear-view mirror was different, and there was a new storage tray on the centre console below the e-brake handle. Then the armrests on the doors were a little larger, and some of the labelling on the dashboard switches had changed to reflect equipment changes. That, believed BMW, was enough.

The Special Editions

The idea of individuality was central to the marketing of the MINI from the beginning, and that long options list enabled buyers to create a specification that they could reasonably believe was special to them. It might not have been unique, but the chance of encountering another car with exactly the same features was remote. From 2005, MINI introduced special editions to increase this element of individuality.

Car makers typically produce special editions of their products to boost flagging sales or to provide a product at a price point where it seems advantageous to explore the sales possibilities. They also use such editions to test market acceptance of new features before introducing them on mainstream models. Typically, special editions are promoted as offering good value for money, with a combination of features that would cost far more if ordered individually as options.

No doubt all these motives influenced the multiple special edition MINIs, but the main reason for their existence was to attract customers who wanted something not only fashionable but also distinctive. BMW held off until June 2005 because the mainstream models were selling so well, and then tested the water with three special editions that were all released at the same time. There was one based on the Mini ONE, one on the Cooper, and one on the Cooper S.

The MINI One Seven was one of the first three special editions, and its name recalled the Austin Seven version of the original Mini, built between 1959 and 1962. It was a MINI One with Solar Red metallic paint (which remained unique) and several desirable items from the options list. There were also special decal badges.

The Cooper derivative of the first three special editions was the Park Lane, named to suggest the expensive and exclusive road in London's West End. It came in Royal Grey metallic paint with a silver roof and bonnet stripes, plus Park Lane decals and another tempting choice of items from the options list.

The scuttle became a favourite place for special-edition identification badges. Here is one on the Checkmate edition. (Detectandpreserve/WikiMedia Commons)

The cumulative effect of several extra cosmetic features made the Sidewalk Convertible a highly distinctive MINI model. (The_Car_Spy/WikiMedia Commons)

The initial trio was completed by the Checkmate, based on a Cooper S. It had a Space Blue metallic body with a silver roof, mirror caps and bonnet stripes, and checkerboard decals behind the front wheel arches. The seats had Checkmate cloth with leather and matching trim, and there were other special detail features.

The Designer's Choice edition from November 2006 was a last-gasp special edition of the first-generation car for the Japanese market, announced just as the second-generation cars were going on sale elsewhere. There were 100 cars based on the Cooper and 200 on the Cooper S, all in Astro Black with a white roof featuring a black graphic showing head-on and profile views of a Cooper.

The April 2007 Sidewalk Convertible was the last special edition based on the first-generation MINI, of which the Hatch models had gone out of production in 2006. It was previewed at the Detroit Motor Show in January 2007 and was designed partly to boost US sales, although it was available as a global special edition and there were 150 for the UK market. This was a Convertible in Deep Laguna metallic, with a black soft top featuring a 'Sidewalk' pattern in Titanium Grey. As usual, it had several special details as well.

Unique interior treatments added to the appeal of the special editions. This is the Sidewalk Convertible again. (The_Car_Spy/WikiMedia Commons)

3

The Second Generation, 2006–2013

BMW had planned for a second generation of its MINI after five years of production, and work began on the new model almost as soon as the first-generation car had reached the showrooms. It was clear from early on that a major reorientation would not be necessary. MINI was already appealing to its target customers very effectively – and in fact the millionth example would be built shortly after the second-generation cars were introduced in November 2006.

The new 2007-model MINI Cooper was easily recognised by changes to the front end, including those prominent indicators within the headlight units.

Each new tail lamp for 2007 contained a white section for the reversing light.

So now was the time to build on that initial success. More modern engineering was in the package, but it was clothed in a bodyshell that looked very much like its predecessor. The novelties came as BMW explored the limits of the MINI's possibilities with variations on the theme. During the production of the first generation, there had been just two body variants: the Hatch and the Convertible. With the second generation, BMW would push the envelope by adding no fewer than six new body variants that were intended to seek out new groups of customers.

One result was a proliferation of code numbers for the second-generation cars. The basic three-door Hatch was an R56 (a code sometimes used as shorthand to describe all the second-generation cars). On top of that, there were R55 (Clubman and Clubvan), R57 (Convertible), R58 (Coupé), R59 (Roadster), R60 (Countryman) and R61 (Paceman) types. These variants are discussed in more detail in the next chapter.

Despite its very similar appearance, the R56 Hatch bodyshell was much changed from its R50 predecessor. There was now no separate designation for the Cooper S; all three model variants were R56 types. The new shell was 60 mm (2.4 in) longer than the old, and to comply with forthcoming new European regulations about pedestrian collisions its

The R56 dashboard followed the theme established by the R50 models and incorporated several retro-styled 'surprise and delight' features.

Door trim panels had a familiar look, with armrests set within large, chunky frames.

bonnet was higher off the ground. This was not easy to see in isolation; more obvious was that the indicators were no longer mounted below the headlamps but within them. The grille was also restyled.

To reduce collision-repair costs, the headlamps were no longer attached to the bonnet itself but to the front quarter-panels. The air scoop in the Cooper S bonnet was now purely cosmetic because the intercooler had been moved to the front of the engine from its earlier position on top of it. Less visibly, the battery was now located more conventionally. The C-pillars were no longer under glass, the rear light clusters were larger than before, and the rear valance contained twin reversing lights flanking a red fog-guard lamp.

Changes to the interior were not immediately obvious, but there was welcome extra room for the rear-seat passengers thanks to hollowed-out backs for the front seats. The dashboard retained its distinctive style with a large circular speedometer in the centre, but the second-generation MINI came with a transponder key fob and instead of a key ignition switch there was a large engine start button. A new and associated option was a keyless entry option called Comfort Access. Meanwhile, the extra size of the shell allowed for a bigger boot.

The Initial Range

With the second-generation MINI came a completely new range of engines. These were the result of a collaboration with PSA Peugeot-Citroen in France, and those for the MINI were built at BMW's new factory at Hams Hall, near Birmingham. Nevertheless, the old Tritec engines remained in production until June 2007, providing a stock for the R52 first-generation convertible that would continue in build alongside the new models until 2009. BMW sold its stake in the Brazilian company to DaimlerChrysler (the brief marriage of Daimler-Benz and Chrysler), and then in early 2008 the plant and the rights to manufacture Tritec engines were sold on to Fiat, who later re-engineered the design to produce their own E-torQ type.

The new MINI petrol engines were known as Prince types, and all had the same 1.6-litre (1,598-cc) capacity as the earlier Tritec engines, in each case with a little more power than the one they replaced. The base engine in the MINI One – which arrived after the other two models, in 2007 – had 98PS with 153Nm (113 lb ft) of torque, while the Cooper's 122PS and 160Nm (118 lb ft) resulted mainly from a different management 'chip'. These engines were known to BMW as N12 types and incorporated the German company's efficient Valvetronic variable camshaft system.

For the Cooper S, however, the engine did not have Valvetronic but depended on a twin-scroll turbocharger (its predecessor had been supercharged) and a direct-injection fuel system. This was known as the N14 type and it delivered 184PS with 240Nm (177 lb ft) developed over a wide range of engine speeds. An overboost feature allowed 260Nm (191 lb ft) over a restricted rev range, with electronic controls to prevent engine damage.

The new diesel engine was another collaborative design, in this case resulting from links between PSA Peugeot-Citroën and Ford of Europe. Peugeot knew it as a DV6 type and Ford as a DLD-416, and it was so much more powerful than the earlier diesel engine in the MINI

The Cooper still had a single exhaust tailpipe, but like the other R56 models had larger tail lights and exposed rear window pillars.

The R56 Cooper S, of course, had a different rear valance with twin tailpipes and fog guard lamps set within that stylish grille.

that BMW decided to align it with the mid-range MINI rather than the entry-level type and launch it in a new model called the Cooper D. Once again a 1,598-cc four-cylinder, it promised 112PS with 270Nm (199 lb ft) of torque, which made for performance that was fully appropriate to the Cooper name.

The Later Models

The second-generation MINI was in production for seven years, and in that time the six new models already mentioned were introduced, plus a seventh in the shape of a second-generation Convertible that replaced the old R52 type. On top of that, the basic range underwent multiple and quite confusing changes.

As already noted, Cooper and Cooper S models arrived first in 2006, and the entry-level MINI One did not arrive until April 2007, at the same time as the Cooper D. Also introduced in 2007 were the new Clubman estate models.

In September 2008, BMW's DSC (Dynamic Stability Control) system was made standard across the range. Two more important introductions followed in 2009, the new MINI First in July and the new R57 Convertible in July. This replaced the old-model MINI Convertible for the 2010 season.

As its name suggested, the MINI First made an ideal first car (for those who could afford one) thanks to its lower-powered engine, a 1.4-litre version of the Prince four-cylinder with just 75PS. The only obvious exterior change was to plastic wheel trims. The First cost less to buy and insure than a MINI One, and offered almost as much driving enjoyment despite its lower top speed of 109 mph and diminished acceleration (0–60 mph took 12.8 seconds). Neither exhaust emissions nor fuel consumption were lower than those of a MINI One despite the presence of a stop-start system, and of course only a six-speed manual gearbox was available. Nevertheless, this was an attractive new addition to the MINI range.

In 2010, the new models were a MINI One D and the Countryman with four doors and all-wheel drive that explored the outer limits of the MINI range. There is more about the Countryman in the next chapter, but the One D was based on the R56 three-door Hatch and provided an entry-level diesel model for economy-minded buyers. It had a lower-powered version of the 1.6-litre Peugeot diesel engine, with just 90PS but 215Nm (158 lb ft) of torque spread over a useful engine speed range.

Minor visual alterations and new diesel engines distinguished the 2011 models announced in June 2010. These had a new front bumper (for better pedestrian protection) with fog lamps on either side of the air intake and, for the Cooper S, air intakes for brake cooling. There were new headlamp elements, new side indicator repeaters and changes to the rear bumper and tail lights, which now had LEDs with a concentric-ring design. There were softer interior materials, too, and a new MINI Connected multimedia system for use with an iPhone. Active headlights and an auto-dimming rear-view mirror joined the options list.

The new 1.6-litre diesel engines belonged to BMW's N47 family and were shared with the BMW 1 Series cars. These lightweight all-aluminium four-cylinders had common-rail direct injection and a variable-vane turbocharger. Stop-start, automatic alternator disengagement, and dashboard gearchange advisories helped reduce fuel consumption and emissions. In the One D, the new diesel had 89 bhp with 159 lb ft of torque and could accelerate to 62 mph (100 km/h) in 11.4 seconds. The Cooper D version came with 112 bhp, 199 lb ft of torque, and a top speed of 122 mph. Acceleration to 62 mph took 9.7 seconds. These engines also became the first diesels offered in a MINI Convertible.

There were no changes to the petrol models at this stage, but the turbocharged N14 engine in the Cooper S had developed a reputation for problems. So during 2011 BMW replaced it with a revised Prince 1.6-litre type called the N18 that featured double-VANOS variable valve timing and also delivered very similar power, with better fuel economy.

This new engine was not the only 2011 change, of course. June brought a new model in the form of the Coupé, and the Paceman followed as a 2012 model later in the year. For some markets, a 2-litre (1,995-cc) version of the N47 diesel engine was now introduced, bringing 111 bhp and 270Nm (171 lb ft) in Cooper D form and 143 bhp with 305Nm (225 lb ft) in Cooper SD form.

Then from January 2012 there was a Roadster that was derived from the Coupé, and the last new model was the Clubvan, derived from the Clubman and designed to take the MINI range in yet another new direction.

The Rocketman Concept

Just as MINIs were starting to get bigger (see Chapter 4) and move further away from the original concept of a small car, so BMW outsmarted public opinion by displaying a new

Just when we thought the MINI was no longer a small car, BMW displayed their Rocketman concept.

model that was actually smaller. They called it the Rocketman concept and showed it at Geneva in March 2011.

The Rocketman was nearly a foot shorter than the F56 Hatch, and some 20 inches shorter than a Clubman. With just two seats (although a 3+1 option was also planned), this was a lightweight city car that was claimed to achieve up to 94mpg – although BMW revealed nothing about its powerplant.

Inevitably some elements of this show car were designed primarily to grab attention. A carbon-fibre space frame was partly visible on the car's exterior and minimised weight; dual-hinged doors gave superb access in confined spaces; and there was a horizontally split tailgate. A trackball on the steering wheel, projector tail lights, and a fibre-optic Union Jack embedded in the roof were all show car features – but not in the realms of fantasy.

The Rocketman was not intended for production. But ten years later, in 2021, it looked as if the ideas behind it were to be resurrected for a new MINI model with electric power that would be produced for the Chinese domestic market in conjunction with carmaker Great Wall.

The Special Editions

Just as they had with the first-generation R50 cars, BMW waited a few years before making special-edition versions of the second-generation models available. The first ones appeared in 2009 and were announced at (or in one case before) the Mini 50th birthday celebrations at Silverstone in May but did not go on sale until August.

The purpose of these special editions was the same as before, and they usually came with special colours or colour combinations, unique details, and an attractive combination of extras taken from the options list. Most were identified by special badges, typically mounted next to the side repeater lamps and on the boot lid, but sometimes elsewhere on the body.

The Graphite was announced just before the 50th Anniversary event, and was less a special edition than a package available on the One, Cooper, and Cooper D models. These cars had Dark Silver metallic paint with black bonnet stripes (One) or a choice of black or white bonnet stripes (Cooper and Cooper D).

The MINI 50 Mayfair was announced at the 50th Anniversary event and could be based on a Cooper, Cooper D or Cooper S. The Mayfair name was familiar from a version of the original Mini available in the 1980s and referred to an expensive and upper-crust area in London's West End. The colour scheme was Hot Chocolate metallic with a white roof, although other colours were available to order. The Mayfair had a twelve-month availability limitation.

The MINI 50 Camden was the third special edition associated with the 50th Anniversary celebrations. Like the other two, it was available only for a twelve-month period. The Camden came as a Cooper, Cooper D or Cooper S, painted White Silver, Midnight Black or Horizon Blue metallic, in each case with a white roof. The bonnet shoulders had a unique silver stripe trim.

The Minimalist model was announced at the Geneva Show in March 2010. It featured a number of items developed under the Minimalism programme, roughly equivalent to BMW's Efficient Dynamics programme to reduce fuel consumption and emissions. These included rather unattractive 'aerodynamically optimised' 15-inch wheels, tyres with a low rolling resistance, and an engine stop-start system. Two different versions were available, with either 75PS or 98PS, depending on the destination country, but always based on the Hatch with a manual gearbox.

Following the lead of the Mayfair and Camden editions, the March 2011 Pimlico was named with a London theme. It was available for only twelve months and came as a MINI One, MINI One D, MINI Cooper, or MINI Cooper D. The paintwork was in Laser Blue metallic.

The Soho edition, based on the Cooper Hatch and Convertible, was released in August 2011 to follow the success of the 2010 Soho Clubman (see Chapter 4) and shared a number of its features. This was another London-themed name, and the Soho could be had in Cooper or Cooper D guise, as a Hatch or a Convertible. It came in White Silver with a black roof and mirror caps.

The Baker Street edition was the less expensive of the two announced in January 2012. It came as a MINI One, One D, Cooper, or Cooper D, in Rooftop Grey metallic,

The Baker Street edition of January 2012 came with an attractive set of distinguishing features...

...and it was hard to take them all in at once. That was part of the appeal of the BMW special editions.

The standard combination of Kite Blue and Black for the MINI Bayswater also brought bonnet stripes and mirror caps that were differently coloured on each side of the car.

with a black roof on the Cooper and Cooper D versions. Alternative body colours were available.

The Bayswater edition was the more expensive of the two announced in January 2012, and was available as a Cooper, Cooper D, Cooper S, or Cooper SD. Standard finish was Kite Blue metallic with a black roof, but the Cooper S and Cooper SD variants could be had in other colours. An interesting new feature was that the bonnet stripe and mirror cap on the right side were blue, while those on the left were grey.

Two more special editions were announced in April 2012. Both Hatch and Clubman variants of the Green Park edition were available, but the exact model mix varied from country to country. There were Cooper, Cooper D, Cooper S and Cooper SD options. All of them came in Pepper White with a British Racing Green roof.

The second April 2012 edition was the Hyde Park, which was also available as both Hatch and Clubman and on the same four base models. Again, the exact model mix varied from country to country. Hyde Park MINIs had Pepper White paint with a Hot Chocolate roof.

BMW's sponsorship of the 2012 Olympics in London offered a golden opportunity for an Olympic-themed special edition MINI, and not surprisingly it was called the Olympic Edition. Based on the Cooper model, 2,012 were built, with a choice of Chili Red, White Silver or Lightning Blue paintwork. In each case, a white roof had the 'London 2012' logo and there were various Union flag features both inside and outside the car.

The Green Park edition came as both Hatch and Clubman, and was another London-themed model.

Much of the appeal of the special-edition MINIs came from specially crafted interiors. This is the one for the Green Park edition.

4

Beyond the Hatch,
2006–2013

All the early first-generation MINIs were three-door Hatch models until the R52 Convertible arrived in July 2004 at the same time as the mid-life facelift. Neither of these models took the MINI range beyond where it had ventured before, because there had been three-door saloon and convertible models of the original Mini.

The original Mini range had also included estate, van and pick-up models, and in due course BMW would explore several of these as extensions of the new MINI range. However, the MINI designers also drew up some entirely unexpected variants during the lifetime of the second-generation models. Not all of them were successful enough to be continued as third-generation models, and as a result the Clubvan, Countryman, Coupé, Paceman and Roadster remained interesting aberrations in the MINI story. This chapter discusses them in the order of their appearance in MINI showrooms around the world, and also looks at the small number of special-edition versions that accompanied them.

Clubman, 2007–2013

After the Convertible in 2004, there were no new body variants until 2007, when the Clubman appeared. This was an estate car with a folding rear seat and, like the estate derivatives of the original MINI, it was built on a longer wheelbase than the standard Hatch. The extra 80 mm (just over 3 inches) of wheelbase allowed more room inside, making this a more practical family model than the Hatch, and adjustments elsewhere added 240 mm (9.4 inches) to the model's length. It was also 64 kg (141 lb) heavier than the Hatch.

The original Mini estates had been called the Countryman and the Traveller, but BMW did not have the rights to those names at the time and instead chose one that they did own, calling the R55 estate a Clubman. That was slightly confusing for anyone familiar with the older Mini, where the Clubman had been a facelifted model with different front

The Clubman body lent itself to eye-catching paint treatment like this, seen on a Cooper S variant. On this side, there was just one side door...

...but on the other side, there were two. The twin tail doors were a deliberate echo of the original Mini estate design.

Interior treatment of the Clubman was entirely familiar; this is a Cooper S model built in 2007.

end panels. Nevertheless, the vertically split tail doors of the original Mini estates were faithfully replicated – clearly indicating that BMW still felt the need to draw on the heritage of the original car.

The R55 Clubman had one other quirk. Although it had two conventional doors on the left, it also had a single smaller door on the right, known as a Clubdoor. This was useful in countries with left-hand drive because it opened onto the kerb side. Unfortunately, the Clubdoor remained on the right for right-hand drive cars, meaning its practical advantages were completely lost.

The original Clubman was available with all the same variants as the MINI Hatch, the single exception being the One Diesel. It sold well enough to be one of the models that would be continued into the third-generation MINI range. This time, however, its appeal to right-hand-drive markets would be improved with conventional doors on both sides.

Convertible, 2009–2013

The second-generation MINI Convertible was previewed at the Detroit and Geneva Motor Shows in early 2009, and reached showrooms that autumn. The new models had stiffer bodyshells than their predecessors, and also incorporated a rollover bar that only deployed when needed. Meanwhile, the new soft top could be opened and closed in fifteen seconds as long as the car was stationary or travelling no faster than 30 km/h (18.6 mph). It also had improved sound-deadening and a glass rear window with a demister element. The boot lid hinges were now concealed, and the boot itself was bigger: between 125 and 170 litres were available when driving with the top down, and this increased to 660 litres with the top up.

An amusing feature of the R57 models was called the Always Open Timer, which recorded how long the car had been driven in open mode – useful for bragging rights, maybe, but otherwise very much a gimmick. The display had its own dial on the dashboard, but was incorporated into the functions of the display screen on the third-generation cars. R57 Convertibles could be had as a MINI One, a Cooper, a Cooper D, a Cooper S, a Cooper SD and a John Cooper Works (see Chapter 6). As on other second-generation MINIs, a six-speed manual gearbox was standard and a six-speed automatic was optional.

Countryman, 2010–2016

The R60 MINI Countryman was a controversial model from the start, introducing all-wheel drive in tandem with a four-door estate bodyshell. Many commentators and enthusiasts argued then – and still do – that it pushed the MINI concept beyond reasonable bounds, and not everybody liked the wrap-over headlamps that came with its redesigned front end. Yet there was no doubt that BMW had understood their market, especially in the USA where the second-generation Countryman went on to account for one in every three MINI sales.

The Countryman explored the possibilities of a small SUV based on the MINI, but was a step too far from the original concept for some. This is an ALL4 version.

Larger tail lights and that distinctive flash leading to the side indicators are clear in this picture. As on other MINI models, the Cooper had a single exhaust tailpipe.

Much of the appeal of the Countryman came from its SUV-like versatility, spearheaded by the large load space seen here.

The Countryman was prompted by the popularity of SUVs (especially in the USA) and has been described as a 'subcompact luxury crossover SUV'. BMW previewed it in concept form at the Paris Show in autumn 2008, when they showed the MINI Crossover Concept with an intriguing arrangement of doors. The two on the right or kerb side in LHD markets were conventional, but on the other side one conventional door was accompanied by a lift-and-slide door that would not interfere with traffic. The production model nevertheless had four conventionally hinged doors when it was announced at the Geneva Show in March 2010.

No production versions of the original Mini had been built with all-wheel drive, and by no means every example of the new MINI Countryman had it either. However, all of them had the taller ride height usually associated with such drive systems, and this was much appreciated because it gave easier passenger and cargo access. When fitted, the four-wheel-drive system was called ALL4, and it depended on an electro-hydraulic differential to vary the power distribution between front and rear wheels. In normal conditions, no more than 50 per cent was distributed to the rear wheels, but when the system's sensors detected a loss of traction it could direct all the power to the rear.

All Countryman models, with or without four-wheel drive, were built by Magna Steyr in Austria. They were thus the first models of the MINI range not to come from the

The tall Countryman gave rise to this MINI Beachcomber Concept, here pictured at the Geneva Show in March 2010. No production followed. (El monty/WikiMedia Commons)

Oxford plant in Britain where other MINIs were made. Model availability varied from one market to another, but the Countryman was initially made in One, One D, Cooper, Cooper D and Cooper D versions, with ALL4 available only for the Cooper D and Cooper S. In spring 2011, a Cooper SD model was added, along with automatic versions of the Cooper D and ALL4 versions of the Cooper SD and Cooper D Automatic, and from July 2013 there was a Cooper ALL4 model as well. In some markets, it was badged as a Crossover.

Unsurprisingly, the Countryman was developed on the back of its success. From November 2012, European models were modified to meet EU6 emissions requirements, and then at the New York motor show in April 2014 a mid-life facelift was announced. This brought a modified hexagonal grille, and under-ride protection for the ALL4 models. The R60 Countryman remained in production until 2017, overlapping with the first models of the new third-generation MINI.

The Countryman also formed the basis of an interesting MINI Beachcomber Concept that was displayed at the Detroit motor show in January 2010 and then again at Geneva in March. This had an ALL4 system but no doors and no fixed roof, and was probably intended to explore the market for a vehicle like the original Mini Moke. However, no production followed.

Coupé, 2011–2015

The R58 Coupé introduced an entirely new model to the MINI range; there had never been a factory-built Coupé variant of the original Mini. It was announced in June 2011, received a public launch at the Frankfurt Show in September, and went on sale after that.

The Coupé was another example of how BMW was pushing the envelope of the MINI range in this period. Some might argue that it was a deliberate attempt to push style at the expense of substance, and it was certainly aimed at the fairly small niche market for a two-seater Coupé, where its main rivals would be the Peugeot RCZ and the VW Scirocco.

It was based on the lower body of a Convertible, but carried a distinctive upper cabin with a more steeply raked windscreen, a roofline lowered by 29 mm (1.1 inches) as compared to a MINI Hatch, and a distinctively shaped roof panel – which to American customers looked like a baseball cap worn backwards. The lower roof made rear seats impractical, and so the back of the passenger cabin was given over to a luggage platform, while some of the space was used to increase the size of the boot to 280 litres. For effect as much as for anything else, the rear of the body carried a spoiler that rose automatically at speeds above 80 km/h (50 mph) or could be deployed manually from a toggle switch above the interior mirror.

The Coupé always had the revised bumpers and interior console layout associated with the second-generation MINI facelift cars. Four models were available – Cooper, Cooper S, Cooper SD and John Cooper Works – and of course base Coupés had the N16 engine while the Cooper S had the turbocharged N18 type.

Coupés were undeniably stylish, but their quite radically sporting looks were not matched by any increases in the performance or handling of their standard Hatch

The R58 Coupé – in this case a Cooper SD model – was a two-seater that was more about style than performance. (nakhon100/WikiMedia Commons)

equivalents. Although less can sometimes be more in the automotive world, the MINI Coupé did not catch the popular imagination and sales were not particularly strong. BMW decided to end production of the model in February 2015, and did not revive the Coupé for the third-generation MINI.

Paceman, 2011–2015

The MINI Paceman was allocated the R61 code, the last one in the second-generation MINI line-up. This was another deliberately niche product from the MINI team that was designed to explore the market for future variants, but proved to be a dead end.

The Paceman was based on the all-wheel-drive platform of the Countryman, and was built alongside it at the Magna Steyr plant in Austria. It was designed as a three-door SUV crossover model, probing the booming market for tall SUV models, and in that respect combined existing MINI features in a way not available in the other variants. It shared the Countryman's front end panels with their wrap-over headlamps, while the rising waistline

The R61 Paceman had a clear styling relationship to the Countryman, but was a more sporty-looking three-door car. This is a Cooper D model with the later 2-litre engine. (Vauxford/ WikiMedia Commons)

The Paceman's rising belt line and narrowing rear side window were featured clearly inspired by the Range Rover Evoque, which had been seen in concept form some years earlier. (Vauxford/ WikiMedia Commons)

and narrowing rear side windows were probably deliberately reminiscent of the newly announced Range Rover Evoque.

Introduced in 2011 as a 2012 model, the Paceman always came in ALL4 guise and with the sporty options of the N16 engine (in the Cooper model) or the turbocharged N18 engine (in the Cooper S). There was a John Cooper Works variant as well. However, the Paceman was quite heavy, and this restricted its performance to some extent; buyers were not impressed by the premium prices that BMW asked for it either.

By late 2014, BMW representatives were publicly saying that the model's days were numbered. The official line was that it was too close to the Countryman model in its appeal and that it would have to go. The MINI Paceman therefore went out of production in 2015 and was not directly replaced in the third-generation MINI line-up.

Clubvan, 2012–2014

There was a long-wheelbase van derivative of the original Mini for much of its life, and the development of a deliberately stylish van from the new MINI was almost inevitable. What became the Clubvan was shown in concept form at Geneva in 2012; a pre-production car followed at that year's Goodwood Festival of Speed, and production began in the autumn.

This was a light van for companies that valued style more than carrying capacity. It had less of that than either the Ford Fiesta or Vauxhall Corsa vans that were its obvious competitors. Essentially, it was a MINI Clubman with body-coloured polycarbonate panels in place of the rear side windows. The inside behind the two front seats was stripped out

The Clubvan was an attractive model, but failed to find enough buyers and was withdrawn after just two years on sale. (Vauxford/WikiMedia Commons)

and fitted with a half-height bulkhead that had a steel mesh upper section, while the load area was fully trimmed and came with lashing points and a pair of 12v power sockets. Paint colours were limited to Black, Blue, Green and White, and the Clubvan could be had with One, One D, Cooper or Cooper D specifications. All models came with the MINImalism efficiency technology.

It was not a huge success, and in Britain suffered from the same problem as the Clubman – that its asymmetric side door arrangement had been designed to suit LHD markets. In the USA, it went on sale early in 2013 but was withdrawn in July after just fifty had been sold because taxation changes priced it out of the market. The last examples were built in 2014.

Roadster, 2012–2015

The R59 MINI Roadster that was introduced in 2012 was very much based on the previous year's Coupé. It had been seen as a concept some three years earlier at the September 2009 Frankfurt Motor Show, but was not formally launched until some months after the Coupé, at the January 2012 Detroit Auto Show. Clearly, BMW anticipated that the new model would find a strong customer base in the USA.

Based on the R58 Coupé, the R59 Roadster was a stylish two-seater that did not catch the imagination of the public and was not carried over to the third-generation MINI.

Like the Coupé, the Roadster was based on the lower body of the Convertible, but it followed the principles of the Coupé in being a two-seater and sharing the more steeply raked windscreen and enlarged boot of the closed car. Its convertible roof was always supplied in black fabric, and came with electric operation in some markets, although it still had to be locked to the windscreen header rail manually. As this was a two-seater car, the fabric roof was designed to cover only the two seats, and therefore consisted of rather less fabric and framework than the one on the four-seater Convertible. It folded down to sit neatly and flush with the top of the body.

Again like the Coupé, the Roadster was designed to push the boundaries of the MINI range and to see what customers might want in future models. Slow sales made clear to BMW that a Roadster was not what they wanted, even though some owners were very enthusiastic about their purchases, and so Roadster production came to an end in 2015. It was not directly replaced among the third-generation MINI line-up.

Special Editions

Just as there were special editions of the mainstream MINI models, so there were special editions of the special models, but there were far fewer of them and some models had no special editions at all.

There were different versions of the Clubman-based Soho special edition for different countries, and the UK market received only one of them (on the Clubman D), between August 2010 and February 2011. There would be a second Soho edition in 2011, this time based on the Hatch and Convertible (see Chapter 3). The UK models came in White Silver with a black roof, but other options were available to order.

The Countryman Rally Edition was unveiled at the Paris Motor Show in October 2010. It was less a special edition than a special variant built in limited numbers. It was developed in association with rally-car specialists Prodrive during 2009, and its 1.6-litre engine was provided by BMW Motorsport. The car was based on the Cooper S ALL4 Countryman.

The Hampton edition of the Clubman was released in March 2011 at the same time as the Pimlico edition of the Hatch, and was displayed at the Geneva Show that month. It was available as a Cooper, Cooper D, Cooper S, or Cooper SD, and all versions had Reef Blue metallic paint with a black roof and Damson Red bonnet stripes.

The February 2012 Highgate came only as a Convertible and was based on a Cooper, Cooper D, Cooper S or Cooper SD. Paintwork was in Iced Chocolate metallic, and the convertible top was in Silver-touched Truffle (brown with a metallic sheen). Other paint options were available to order.

The KISS Edition was a very special edition produced for the USA in collaboration with the rock band KISS and announced at the New York Auto Show. Four different paint finishes were devised for the Countryman models, each one based on the face paint associated with one member of the band. The four original cars on which the paint schemes had been prototyped were sold at a special Father's Day eBay charity auction on 29 May 2011, and the proceeds of $129,000 were donated to UNICEF. Meanwhile, from 21 April, MINI USA sold vehicle wraps with these designs for Countryman models through

The 2011 Hampton special edition added extra style to the Clubman models.

The contrasting black roof is not easy to see in this rear view of a Hampton, but the post-2010 rear body revisions are clear.

The 2012 Highgate edition was based on the R57 Convertible. This was a deliberately smart-looking model designed to appeal to urban dwellers.

their dealerships and web site. All proceeds from the sales of these were also donated to UNICEF, specifically to help children in Japan affected by the Tohoku earthquake and tsunami that had occurred on 11 March. 'Our hearts go out to the people of Japan in this time of great tragedy. We wanted to help and also to provide a real way for the KISS Army to get involved,' said Gene Simmons, the frontman of KISS.

Clubman versions of the Green Park and Hyde Park special editions were announced in April 2012 alongside equivalents based on the Hatch. The specifications of these models are shown in Chapter 3.

The Bond Street special edition based on the Clubman was announced at the Geneva Motor Show in March 2013 and was available only for a limited period. Base models were the Cooper, Cooper D, Cooper S and Cooper SD, in each case painted Midnight Black metallic, with the roof and lower C-pillars in Cool Champagne.

As on so many special editions, the Highgate had specially branded door sills.

Rock band Kiss lent their name to a series of 'wraps' derived from the four Countryman prototypes seen here with band members in full stage make-up.

The interior of one of the four Kiss prototype models is seen here.

The Hyde Park edition of 2012 was one of many with names linked to London. This is the Clubman version; there was a Hatch as well.

Above: The Bond Street edition of the Clubman arrived in 2013, with Midnight Black paintwork set off by Cool Champagne roof and body pillars.

Right: The area next to the side repeater indicators was a favourite for special-edition identification badges.

5

The Third Generation, from 2013

A major change in BMW's approach to the MINI range became very obvious when the third-generation models were introduced in November 2013. The first two generations had been treated as very separate from their BMW-branded contemporaries, but it now appeared to be BMW policy to integrate the MINI more closely into the parent company.

None of this was obvious in the appearance of the cars, which looked much like their predecessors. Under the skin, however, they were built on BMW's latest modular platforms. Some were on the UKL (Untere KLasse or small-car) platform that was unique to the MINI, but the long-wheelbase models were on the UKL2 platform that was shared with BMW's 1-series and 2-series ranges. Even the model codes now had a BMW ring to them. Instead of the earlier R-prefix codes originally established for Rover products, the third-generation models used F-prefix codes like other models from BMW. The first ones released were the F55 (a new five-door Hatch), F56 (the three-door Hatch) and F57 (the Convertible).

Modernisation was apparent in the interiors, too. Although there was still a large round central display on the dashboard, it no longer contained the speedometer. That was now ahead of the driver, and the large central display was a multi-function screen that controlled operation of the car's multiple convenience features.

The new F56 generation (it is often familiarly described by the code for the core Hatch model) had a completely new range of engines, all designed and manufactured by BMW. They had a modular design and came as both three-cylinder and four-cylinder types, and with a great deal of commonality between the petrol and diesel versions. All had an alloy cylinder block, with Valvetronic valve control and a single turbocharger, and several would be shared with BMW-branded models.

The three-cylinder petrol engines were B38 types, and for the MINI they came in sizes of 1.2 litres and 1.5 litres. The three-cylinder diesel was a B37 type, with just a 1.5-litre size. Their four-cylinder relatives were the B47 diesel and the B48 petrol engines, each with a 2-litre capacity. In each case, juggling with engine control systems and other items produced engines of different power outputs from the same capacity. Beyond the

Examples of the 2014-model F56 Cooper (left) and F56 Cooper S display the new 'face' of the third-generation MINI.

Still recognisably MINI, this Cooper shows that the car was beginning to look larger, as well as heavier.

MINI range, six-cylinder petrol engines of the B58 family with the same architecture would power BMW models.

This closer integration with other BMW products was a result of a drive for economies of scale and simpler manufacturing logistics. Only by sharing platforms and other major components could BMW keep control of costs and complexity. In a nutshell, the MINI's individuality had to be sacrificed to save money. Yet BMW was determined to hang on to as much of that individuality as it possibly could, and for customers who did not enquire into the technical side of the third-generation models – which was most of them – it was very much business as usual.

The MINI's success certainly had been extraordinary. From an initial output of 300 cars a day in 2001, the Oxford plant had increased its productivity until it was building 1,000 cars a day in 2019. BMW publicity pointed out that the Oxford workforce were then producing one new MINI every sixty-seven seconds, and that in the previous year nearly 400,000 MINIs had been sold in 110 countries around the world.

This was no longer the cosy British operation with which the MINI brand had started; it was now an international operation serving a genuinely global market. Even though the Oxford plant remained the hub of MINI production, it had for some years not been the only plant building MINIs. Expansion into overseas plants had begun in 2010 when Countryman production was farmed out to contract manufacturer Magna Steyr at Graz in Austria.

The 10 millionth Mini (of which 4.7 million were of the BMW variety) left the assembly lines at Plant Oxford on 9 August 2019.

The global success of that model had prompted further expansion, and during 2013 three BMW assembly plants became involved with its manufacture, each serving its own local market. From April 2013, Countryman assembly started up at Chennai in India; in June, the plant at Kulim in Kedah, Malaysia, followed suit; and in August these two were joined by the Rayong plant in Thailand. Just under a year later, in July 2014 the production lines for global Convertible production were moved to the VDL Nedcar plant at Born in the Netherlands. There was simply not enough room at Oxford any more.

Nevertheless, the Oxford plant was still seen as the spiritual home of the MINI, and when the 10 millionth car was built (the total included 5.3 million examples of the original Mini) on 9 August 2019, the occasion was celebrated at Oxford. The car was a MINI 60 special edition because the brand was then celebrating six decades since its birth in 1959.

The Models

As the third-generation MINI came on-stream in 2013, the model line-up consisted of the entry-level First, the One, the Cooper and the Cooper S, and all of them except the First could be ordered with either a petrol or a diesel engine. There was still a choice between manual and automatic gearboxes, except in the entry-level First that always came with a manual gearbox.

There was still no mistaking a Cooper S, with its centrally placed twin exhaust outlets.

The core model was still the three-door Hatch, but in addition there were Convertible models, Clubman estate models and the Countryman compact SUV with its ALL4 option. In practice, the third-generation or F60 Countryman would not arrive until 2017, when there was a major realignment of the range, and the second-generation R60 Countryman held the fort very ably until then.

As always, it took some concentration to grasp the variety of engine options. The entry-level MINI First had just 75PS from its 1.2-litre turbocharged three-cylinder, but the MINI One had a 102PS version of the same engine. The three-cylinder Cooper engine delivered 136 bhp, and the four-cylinder Cooper S power plant with its 2-litre capacity had 192 bhp. The new diesel models reached showrooms in March 2014, a little after their petrol counterparts. Here, the 1.5-litre three-cylinder gave 95PS for the entry-level models or 116PS for the Cooper D.

Then from 2015, as Chapter 6 explains, there would be a new marketing push behind high-performance derivatives, and the JCW (John Cooper Works) model would become the performance flagship of the range with an even more powerful derivative of the Cooper S engine.

The Five-door Hatch

Although many of the niche models built during the lifetime of the second-generation MINI had been discontinued, BMW continued to explore opportunities for expanding the range. So it was that a five-door Hatch model was announced in June 2014 and went on sale that autumn, with the usual variety of engine options.

The F55 five-door MINI went on sale as a 2015 model to give the MINI more appeal as family transport. It was like a MINI – but bigger. This is a Cooper D model.

The five-door or F55 model was of course designed to offer extra room in the back and extra doors for access to it. To that end, it was built on a longer platform than the three-door Hatch, with an extra 72 mm (2.8 inches) in the wheelbase and an overall increase in length of 161 mm (6.3 inches). Some of that extra length allowed for a larger boot, and a 60/40 split-fold rear seat gave even more carrying capacity when folded forwards. The concept was faultless, but the reality not quite as deserving of praise, and *Autocar* magazine pointed out that the rear doors were rather narrow and legroom in the back was not generous.

Nevertheless, it still looked like a MINI – unsurprisingly, like a three-door Hatch with an extra pair of doors inserted into the middle. It also handled and performed like one 'in almost every respect ... like the three-door model we drove earlier this year,' reported *Autocar* after trying a Cooper D model.

The Superleggera Vision Concept

In May 2014, at the prestigious annual Concorso D'Eleganza held at the Villa d'Este on Lake Como in Italy, BMW revealed the Superleggera Vision Concept. This was another fascinating exploration of the boundaries of the MINI range.

The MINI Superleggera Vision Concept of 2014 indicated one direction the brand might take in the future.

The Superleggera was a hugely attractive roadster with its minimalist lines designed by Anders Warming, then Head of MINI Design, and (as its name suggested) was built at the Superleggera coachworks in Italy.

There were rumours that it would become a production model, but by 2021 no production car had emerged.

Countryman and PHEV

With the new F60 Countryman, introduced in October 2016, the appearance of the largest MINI was vastly improved. Though instantly recognisable as a MINI Countryman, the F60 looked more rugged and had a more coherent design. Careful changes also made it look lower than the model it replaced, although it was not, and new headlamps with squarer frames very much improved the front end appearance. There were some engine changes for the range at the same time, as the four-cylinder 2-litre diesel brought 150PS for the Cooper D ALL4 models and 190PS for the Cooper SD types.

The new Countryman became an F60 when it appeared in 2017 with a much more mature design than the R60 it replaced. This is the PHEV version; note the yellow 'plug' symbol on the tailgate.

Less than a year later, MINI announced a very special version of the F60 Countryman as its first step on the road towards a production electric MINI. This was not yet an all-electric model but a PHEV (Plug-In Hybrid Electric Vehicle) that combined the Cooper's 134 bhp two-stage turbocharged three-cylinder engine with an 87 bhp electric motor. The hardware of the ALL4 drivetrain worked with a sophisticated control system that switched automatically between the two sources of power. The petrol engine drove the front wheels through a six-speed Steptronic automatic gearbox, while the electric motor drove the rear wheels through a single-speed transmission.

This powertrain specification was closely similar to that of the BMW 2 Series Active Tourer Hybrid, and the location of the lithium-ion battery pack under the rear seat meant that the sliding mechanism for the seat base had to be omitted. A smaller petrol tank made room for the electric motor, which also took up some of the boot space, and the electric components added around 150 kg (330 lb) to the overall weight of the car. Even so, the hybrid MINI could reach 123 mph and, with the petrol and electric engines working in tandem, could accelerate to 62 mph (100 km/h) in 6.8 seconds.

BMW claimed that the battery alone could provide a range of up to 26 miles, although some British road tests could not better a 15–20 mile range. Nevertheless, the standard regenerative braking system (which recharged the battery through kinetic energy from braking) helped to keep the batteries well charged, and to make this halfway house between internal combustion and electric power easy to use.

In Britain, the PHEV model was previewed at the prestigious Goodwood Festival of Speed in June 2017. An announcement geared to US customers then followed at the 2018 New York International Show. After that show, three specially equipped Countryman Panamericana models demonstrated the reliability of the new PHEV technology by driving the 25,750 km Pan-American Highway from North America to Tierra del Fuego.

DCT and Facelift

From late 2017, there was also a gradual introduction of new seven-speed Dual Clutch Transmissions (DCT) in place of the older six-speed automatics on most models. This was really part of the planned LCI (Life Cycle Impulse, or facelift) for the whole range, of which more became clear early the following year. Yet this was a limited overhaul and a second-stage facelift was planned for 2021.

Only minor visual changes were apparent when the LCI cars were displayed at the Detroit motor show in January 2018. New paint colours and new alloy wheel styles were only to be expected, and the most obvious changes were new LED lights front and rear. The headlights not only looked different behind the glass, but could be replaced at extra cost by a new matrix LED type that came with automatic adjustment and automatic dipping. At the rear, meanwhile, all tail lights took on a Union flag lens design. The Chrome Line package of trims around the lights and grille on earlier MINIs now gave way to a piano black exterior pack. Also new were 2D Mini logos in place of the original 3D type.

Not much was done to the powertrains, although the MINI One switched from the 1.2-litre engine to a 1.5-litre size, which brought 103PS and worthwhile extra torque. Several minor revisions were introduced across the range, but without affecting either performance or efficiency, and even a switch to twin turbochargers for the Cooper D engine made no change to its output. Meanwhile, a final stage in the transmission revisions was that the automatic option for the Cooper SD and JCW models became a new eight-speed Steptronic type; the DCT at this stage had a torque capacity limitation that made it unsuitable for use with their engines.

Inside the passenger cabin, the main news was a multifunction steering wheel, with a 6.5-inch colour display in the centre of the dashboard. The Navigation Plus package brought a larger screen and a variety of convenience features, and there was a new Piano Black interior trim option. Inevitably, the personalisation options were increased as well, and a highlight was that customers could add their own personal touch by means of laser-engraved or 3D-printed dashboard inserts (which of course could become an embarrassment when it was time to sell the car).

The F60 Countryman models were facelifted in May 2020, the most obvious exterior features being new LED head, fog and tail lights, and a new radiator grille with distinctive differences of detail between the various models. There were Cooper, Cooper S and Cooper D variants, each one available with the ALL4 all-wheel-drive option, and again there was a Cooper SE ALL4 PHEV. The standard wheels had 16-inch and 17-inch sizes, but there were options as large as 19 inches. F60 models also took on the new digital dash from the MINI Electric, which is also described in Chapter 7.

The TwinPower Turbo Technology with two-stage turbocharging seen earlier on the four-cylinder diesel engines was now extended to the two petrol engines as well, and

With the revisions for the 2021 season – the MINI's 20th – came a greater reliance on the latest TwinTurbo power BMW engines.

More and more performance, equipment and luxury – yet still a MINI. This 2021-model Cooper S Hatch was pictured at Plant Oxford, home of the MINI.

all engines met the tighter 2020 Euro 6d emissions standards. Transmissions remained 8-speed Steptronic types on the Cooper models, while lower-powered MINI models still came with six-speed manual or seven-speed DCT gearboxes.

...And A New Direction

Although these incremental improvements to the third-generation MINIs ensured that the cars would remain as popular as ever, there was no doubt that BMW were looking way beyond the lifetime of the F56 cars by the time the MINI reached its twentieth anniversary in spring 2021. In fact, its eyes were set on an electric future, and an Electric MINI had entered production more than a year earlier at Plant Oxford. Its story is told in Chapter 7 of this book.

Special Editions

Special editions of the F56 MINI range began to appear in earnest in 2015, but before that there was one very special edition that went on sale in spring 2012. Called Inspired by Goodwood, it was previewed at the Shanghai Motor Show in April 2011 and was intended to tap into the Chinese market for luxury small cars. Nevertheless, it went on sale worldwide as a limited edition of 1,000 cars, based on the Cooper S but painted and trimmed using materials from Rolls-Royce (which, like MINI, was owned by BMW).

The Challenge 210 of March 2015 was a limited edition of 210 cars that celebrated the latest MINI Challenge racing formula, and aimed to bring a racetrack feel to the road car. It was based on a Cooper S with the latest JCW engine boasting 210PS (207 bhp), and featured an exhaust cut-out controlled by Bluetooth that gave a deep, throaty sound (which, sadly, exceeded legal limits for road use).

The Park Lane edition of July 2015 was based on the Countryman and was available with four engine options. Paintwork combined Earl Grey metallic with an Oak Red roof, and the Park Lane had an ALL4 visual package, with Park Lane badges and 19-inch alloy wheels.

February 2016 brought a genuine limited-edition MINI called the Open 150, of which just 150 were built. This was a Cooper S Convertible, with Melting Silver paintwork and a Union flag graphic embroidered on the roof.

The Seven special edition was announced to the press in May 2016 and revealed in public at the Goodwood Festival of Speed in June. This was the second special edition to carry the name, the earlier one dating from June 2005. It came as a three-door or a five-door

The Challenge 210 edition came not only with extra performance but also with special stripes to advertise it.

Hatch, on Cooper, Cooper D, Cooper S and Cooper SD base models. The standard finish was Lapisluxury Blue with a silver roof, but more mundane options could be had to order.

The 2017 model Cooper S Works 210 was released for the UK market as a three-door Hatch with a one-year availability limit. However, its popularity was such that the package was extended to Convertible and five-door models as well after that year was up. These cars were pre-prepared at the factory and then completed by dealers, who fitted a John Cooper Works engine with the cut-out exhaust system.

Released in April 2018, the 1499GT model was a remarkable combination of MINI One (with 1,499-cc engine) and the Sport chassis option that was standard on the JCW models. Just 1,499 examples were built, all three-door Hatches with the JCW aero styling kit. The name was chosen to evoke the 1275GT model of the original Mini that had replaced the original Mini Cooper.

The 25th Anniversary Convertible limited edition of 300 cars was available from May 2018 only in the UK, where it celebrated twenty-five years since the launch of the original Mini convertible in June 1993. It was a Cooper S convertible in Starlight Blue, with white bonnet stripes and mirror caps, a Union Jack embroidered on the roof fabric, and grey leather upholstery.

The 60 Years model was a global special edition that went on sale in March 2019. The UK took 500 examples, all based on the Cooper S Hatch in British Racing Green with a black roof.

There were just 300 examples of the 25th Anniversary Convertible, which looked magnificent in Starlight Blue with contrasting interior.

Left: The 25th Anniversary model also featured a novelty: an embroidered Union flag on its convertible roof.

Below: To celebrate the six decades since the original Mini went on sale, there was a MINI 60 Years edition in 2019.

Celebrating the achievements of Paddy Hopkirk, an edition named after him went on sale in November 2020. Hopkirk had won the 1964 Monte Carlo Rally with a Mini Cooper S, and the Chili Red and white paint scheme of this edition roughly approximated to that of the rally-winning car. Each door also carried the original car's rally number of 37.

Above: The all-black interior of a 60 Years model was typical of the third-generation style, with a large screen in the centre of the dash and the speedometer ahead of the driver.

Right: The Paddy Hopkirk edition even carried the great driver's signature on the left-hand bonnet stripe.

...And Some in the USA

The marketing of the third-generation MINI in the USA called for some special editions unique to that country. Typical were the Starlight Edition, released in 2018 as a Cooper S Clubman in Starlight Blue metallic with a Melting Silver roof and bonnet stripes, and the Yin Yang Edition, from December the same year. This was a Cooper S Countryman in either Midnight Black with a Light White roof, or Light White with a Midnight Black roof, all enhanced by a selection of items from the options list.

6

JCW – The John Cooper Works Models

The sporting heritage of the original Mini depended very much upon the achievements of the Mini Cooper models. The car was regularly successful in track events, but gained international renown when a Cooper S driven by Paddy Hopkirk and Henry Liddon won the Monte Carlo Rally in 1964. Minis triumphed at Monte Carlo in 1965 and 1967 too.

The Mini Cooper had been developed in 1961 from the standard model by John Cooper, a friend of Mini designer Alec Issigonis, who saw the car's potential for competition. BMC, maker of the Mini, turned his work into a production car and paid him a royalty for every one they sold with his name on it.

Fast forward now to the late 1990s, when the BMW MINI was under development. BMW very much wanted to trade on the Cooper heritage, and gained John Cooper's agreement for the use of his name on their more performance-oriented models. Sadly, Cooper himself died in 2000, before the new MINI went on sale, but his son Mike Cooper was now running the family business and worked with BMW to produce an additional high-performance 'halo' conversion that was announced in November 2001.

Buyers of this conversion had to take their cars to the John Cooper Works premises in Sussex for the work to be done; this was a separate business that Mike Cooper had established to deal with the MINI work. The conversion was known simply as the John Cooper Works MINI, and was fully approved by BMW. It depended on a special cylinder head that raised the compression ratio and was gas-flowed and polished in the traditional way. In tandem with a free-flow air filter system and a redesigned stainless steel rear exhaust, the conversion promised 132 bhp, sharper accelerator response and a sportier-sounding exhaust.

Of course, once the higher-performance Cooper S had reached the market, the team at John Cooper Works developed a performance conversion for that. This new conversion was developed so that MINI dealers could fit it, and went on sale in April 2003. With cylinder head, supercharger, exhaust and ECU changes, the JCW Tuning Kit resulted in an engine that delivered 200 bhp. Special badges came with it, and 18-inch wheels were an

In the beginning, John Cooper Works produced conversions of the standard cars. Pictured at the San Francisco Show in November 2004 is an early example, with the 210PS engine and 140-mph top speed – but no special badges yet. (Broken Sphere/WikiMedia Commons)

option, but this remained a fully driveable road car with the sort of individual features that MINI owners had come to love.

During this early period, BMW carefully monitored demand for the JCW conversions, and it seems likely that the plan had always been to take them in-house if the amount of business they generated warranted such a move. The first step in this direction became clear in late 2005, when it became possible to order a Cooper S with the JCW upgrade fitted at the factory rather than by a dealer. John Cooper Works had meanwhile stopped offering the Cooper conversions themselves, and during 2004 introduced what they called a Sound Kit. This added a remapped ECU, a special air intake system, and a less-restrictive cat-back exhaust to the standard Cooper to produce a more aggressive sound and deliver extra performance as well.

BMW proceeded cautiously towards its ultimate aim, which probably always was to develop the JCW theme until it became recognised as the top 'factory' performance option for the MINI – a MINI equivalent of the M badge associated with BMW's own Motorsport division. One step in that direction was the construction of special racing models for the JCW Challenge track events (see sidebar on p. 87), which helped create the image that BMW wanted. On the back of these, BMW developed a special edition in 2006. Called the John Cooper Works GP, this was a limited-volume road-going edition of the race cars that reached the market just before the changeover from first-generation to second-generation MINI. There is more about it, and its successors, below. Its success gave the green light to the next moves in the BMW strategy: in 2007, the German company bought the rights to the John Cooper Works name and in 2008 bought Mike Cooper's company as well.

The GP Models

Legendary within the story of the John Cooper Works cars have been three JCW GP limited-edition cars that were created as road-going equivalents of the race cars developed for the JCW Challenge race series. The first model arrived in 2006, the second in 2012, and the third in 2020. All three are rare versions of the MINI that offer high performance with track-like handling precision to deliver an exciting driving experience.

The 2006 John Cooper Works GP
There were 2,000 of these cars for worldwide consumption, of which just 500 were sold in the UK. They became available in mid-2006, just as the first-generation (R53) cars were about to be replaced.

These models were based on the Cooper S but had a higher-revving engine with modified injectors, intake system and ECU. This delivered 218PS and a top speed of 140 mph with a 0–60 mph time of 6.3 seconds. Like the race cars, they had no rear seats but a strut brace that made the bodyshell stiffer to improve handling. Showroom appeal was aided by several cosmetic touches, such as 18-inch alloy wheels, but the large rear spoiler was genuinely effective at high speeds and had been proven in a wind tunnel.

The 2013 GP2
The John Cooper Works GP2 special edition was introduced in 2012 as a 2013 model. As with the first GP edition, it was limited to 2,000 examples worldwide. The UK took 288 of these, and the USA had 400.

These cars were based on the standard John Cooper Works Hatch, with its turbocharged N18 engine. A raised compression ratio boosted power to 218 bhp (or 214 bhp for the USA), and the performance claimed was 150 mph with a 0–60 mph time of 6.1 seconds. Like the earlier GP edition, the cars had a bodyshell that was stiffened by a strut brace where the rear seats would otherwise be, and they also had an under-bonnet brace.

More precise handling came from lowered, adjustable coil-over suspension with high-performance dampers, and all the cars had bespoke tyres. The front wheels had six-piston Brembo brakes (as used in the BMW 135i), and the ESP stability control system had a special performance-oriented GP setting.

The GP2 had some very distinctive visual features, too, including a full valance tray, a functional rear diffuser and a spoiler with carbon-fibre insert mounted on the hatch. All cars were painted in Thunder Grey with a red frame to the bonnet scoop, red mirror caps

100 per cent approved used – and still expensive! This GP2 model was pictured in a British showroom. (Vauxford/WikiMedia Commons)

and red brake ducts, and special side stripes with the GP logo. There were 17-inch four-spoke alloy wheels, and the cabin featured Recaro sports seats with Anthracite upholstery.

The 2020 GP3

The GP edition of the third-generation MINI was trailed in concept form at the Frankfurt Show in autumn 2017 but was not made available until July 2020. This time, the worldwide total was increased to 3,000 examples, of which 575 were destined for the UK.

The basic formula was the same as before, with stiffer, bespoke suspension settings, a rear strut brace instead of a rear seat, and an uprated engine. The turbocharged four-cylinder B48 engine came with a larger twin-scroll turbocharger than standard, high-flow injectors, and a lower compression ratio to prevent detonation. Power was up to 306PS (302 bhp), the top speed was now 164 mph, and the 0–100 km/h (62 mph) time was down to 5.2 seconds. This was achieved with the standard eight-speed automatic gearbox that was the only transmission option. Handling was assisted by tracks that were 40 mm (1.6 in) wider than standard and by a limited-slip differential.

All these cars came in metallic Racing Grey, with a Melting Silver roof. There was a functional rear spoiler, special JCW mirror caps, and contrast elements in the black hood scoop, door handles and fuel filler lid. The 18-inch alloy wheels also had GP-branded centre caps. Inside the passenger cabin, the seats were in Dinamica leather with GP badges, the steering wheel was leather-bound, and there were further logos on the floor mats.

The MINI brand has followed the example of its BMW parent with regular 'tease' concepts at motor shows. This was the JCW GP Concept shown at Frankfurt in 2017. (Alexander Migl/WikiMedia Commons)

In some markets, the standard, stripped-out version of the car could be equipped at extra cost with a GP Touring Pack that added automatic air conditioning, seat heating and the Navigation Plus Pack.

Second-generation JCW Conversions

The second-generation MINI became available in 2006, and in 2007 a new tuning kit was made available for MINI dealers to install. The host Cooper S models of course now had a completely different engine from before, with a turbocharger instead of a supercharger, and so the kit was quite different. It nevertheless focused once again on the intake system, the ECU and the exhaust. It increased power of the N14 engine to 192 bhp and gave a top speed of 144 mph. There was much-improved in-gear acceleration from a torque increase, and cars with this JCW conversion took 6.8 seconds to accelerate to 62 mph (100 km/h). MINI enthusiasts today often call this the Stage 1 Kit, although that name was never used by JCW themselves or by BMW.

Inevitably, the JCW kit had to be adapted to suit the different characteristics of the N18 engine with its double-VANOS system that was introduced when the range was overhauled in 2011, but in practice the new JCW kit was not available until part-way through the 2012 season. The changes were once again to the inlet and exhaust systems and to the ECU, and

Mean, moody and magnificent! This is a 2011 JCW car, now with the John Cooper Works badge just visible on the grille below the bumper. (Elmschrat/WikiMedia Commons)

this time the peak power went up to 197 bhp. Pandering to the tastes of MINI Owners, these kits also came with JCW emblems to mount on the front and rear of the car, and with a numbered plate mounted on the modified engine.

The Line-built John Cooper Works Models

Meanwhile, a change of focus had become apparent at the Geneva Show in March 2008, when BMW previewed the MINI John Cooper Works. No longer a performance kit, this was instead an additional model in its own right, positioned above the Cooper S in the line-up. It became available through MINI showrooms as a 2009 model.

The first John Cooper Works model was available in both R56 Hatch and R55 Clubman forms, and central to its appeal was a 207 bhp (210PS) version of the turbocharged engine that delivered a 0–100 km/h (62 mph) acceleration time of 6.3 seconds in the Hatch and 6.6 seconds in the heavier Clubman. The extra power (and torque) had been achieved by a new turbocharger allied to a remapped ECU and a bigger-bore exhaust system.

To match the additional power and performance, the JCW models came with four-piston Brembo front brakes acting on perforated and grooved ventilated discs, plus larger rear discs with single-piston calipers. In line with contemporary trends, the calipers on all four wheels were painted red, and the front pair carried a JCW logo as well. Then, for the benefit

This JCW aero kit was pictured on a Cooper S Hatch. (Emilianob66/WikiMedia Commons)

of driving enthusiasts, there was an electronic limited-slip differential, which could vary the locking between zero and 50 per cent and was not confined to the fixed 30 per cent value of the optional LSD on the Cooper S. This feature was known as EDLC, which stood for Electronic Differential Lock Control.

The 2009 John Cooper Works model was also the first MINI to come as standard with DTC (Dynamic Traction Control), as fitted to contemporary BMW models. DTC replaced the DSC (Dynamic Stability Control) available on other MINIs, and its main benefit was to allow a more sporty drive through remapping the parameters for the traction and stability control systems while still ensuring that they operated in extreme circumstances.

These first regular-production John Cooper Works cars of course remained available until the end of the second-generation models' lifetime, when they were replaced by a new model based on the third-generation cars. In the meantime, BMW had explored the sales possibilities further with a special edition and an expansion of the JCW brand to cover the strong-selling Countryman models, as well as the Hatch.

The John Cooper Works World Championship 50 edition was released in August 2009 to celebrate two anniversaries – fifty years of the Mini and fifty years since John Cooper's

The JCW specification was not only available on the Hatch models. This R59 Coupé pictured when new at a US dealership displays the distinctive badge on its lower front apron. (Mr.choppers/WikiMedia Commons)

Also in the USA, this is a MINI Clubman with the JCW treatment. (Flickr)

Above: This 2013 Paceman has both the special grille badge and distinctive side stripes. (Vauxford/WikiMedia Commons)

Left: A second Paceman with the JCW specification, this time pictured at a dealership in Germany. (Thomas Doerfer/WikiMedia Commons)

Formula 1 racing team won its first championship. The model had been previewed at the Mini brand's 50th birthday celebrations in May 2009, and just 250 were built for global consumption. Of these, 100 were for Britain and fifty for the USA. This was a very expensive special edition that cost over £10,000 more than its standard-production equivalent in Britain. '£33k for a Mini – any Mini – is frankly ludicrous,' sniffed *Autocar* magazine in November 2009.

The World Championship 50 cars were of course a finely judged confection in typical MINI special-edition style. Based on Cooper S models, they were all painted in Connaught Green with a white roof, and had white bonnet stripes, the right-hand one signed by Mike Cooper (using his father's name). Jet Black alloy wheels provided a contrast, along with carbon-fibre highlights on the bonnet scoop, the mirror caps, and on the tailgate above the registration plate. Xenon headlights had black internals and the driving lamps had black backs, while there was a special edition number in each side indicator frame. A look inside revealed black leather upholstery with red trim highlights, and a leather-and-alcantara steering wheel. There were more carbon fibre trim elements, a plaque with the special edition number on the centre console, and a Harmon/Kardon stereo system.

The second expansion of the JCW brand was heralded by the appearance of a John Cooper Works Countryman at the Geneva Motor Show in March 2012. This was followed a month later by an appearance at the New York Auto Show. The production car was based on the Cooper S ALL4 version of the Countryman, and was in effect a compact performance SUV with particular appeal to US customers. With the latest 218PS John Cooper Works engine, plus some changes to the steering and suspension, it remained in production until 2016.

The Third-generation Cars

The third-generation MINI was introduced in November 2013, although, as Chapter 5 explains, only some models were available in the initial release. One of those held over for later was a new John Cooper Works car, which arrived in May 2015. It came only as a three-door Hatch.

The JCW version of the four-cylinder Cooper S engine was tuned to deliver 228 bhp and offered a broad spread of extra torque as well with a 23 per cent increase at its peak. Different pistons, a higher boost pressure and a remapped ECU were accompanied by additional cooling ancillaries and a sports exhaust system tuned for aural effect. An electronic differential lock helped put the torque down more evenly, and of course the car had the optional Sports suspension available on the Cooper S, plus more powerful Brembo brakes than were standard on that car.

Interestingly, all the first examples of the 2015 JCW had an eight-speed automatic gearbox, adapted to suit the engine's characteristics, and BMW explained that this had entered production first to meet demand in the major MINI markets of Japan and the USA. A six-speed manual arrived a couple of months later, and MINI Public Relations people expected that 80 per cent of British sales would be of the manual model. Bizarrely, the manual car was not only slightly thirstier than the automatic, but was also slower (by about 0.2 seconds) to 100 km/h. The automatic model's time of 6.1 seconds was of course helped a little by a Launch Control system that limited wheelspin to the benefit of traction. A 153-mph top speed was claimed.

A more aggressive-looking front end incorporated extra air intakes to improve engine cooling, and dispensed with the fog lights standard on the Cooper S. Wheels came with a 17-inch size as standard, but 18-inch alloys with run-flat tyres were an extra-cost option. Meanwhile, there was the usual collection of special features for the interior: special door sills, sports front seats, a three-spoke multifunction steering wheel, a special gear lever, stainless steel pedals and revised instrument graphics.

This third-generation JCW model is a Clubman, and was pictured at a dealership in Japan. (Tokumeigakarinoaoshima/WikiMedia Commons)

This JCW Clubman at the 2019 Frankfurt Show previewed the Union flag tail light graphics. (Alexander Migl/WikiMedia Commons)

Capitalising on these latest developments, BMW announced a very low-volume limited edition called the John Cooper Works Challenge, which was a stripped-out model with the 228 bhp engine, adjustable suspension (as used in racing), special tyres and a stiff purchase price.

In Japan, the name Crossover is used instead of Countryman, but the JCW badge remains the same. (Tokumeigakarinoaoshima/WikiMedia Commons)

Subtle interior touches are part of the modern JCW package, seen here on an F60 Crossover (Countryman) in Japan. (Tokumeigakarinoaoshima/WikiMedia Commons)

Special Editions of the Third-generation JCW

The 2015 Challenge and 2017 Cooper S Works 210 special editions discussed in Chapter 6 paved the way for some special editions of the John Cooper Works model itself, but these were made available only in the USA. They were quite separate from the limited-production GP models, which are discussed in the sidebar on p. 76.

Both reached the market as 2019 models, and followed the usual special-edition formula of extra equipment and individual cosmetic schemes. The earlier of the two had the cumbersome name of John Cooper Works International Orange Edition and was based on the three-door Hatch with, as its name suggested, orange paintwork. Dark contrasts came

Left: Looking the part: this was the JCW Knights special edition for the USA.

Below: This second US 'special' from 2018 was the John Cooper Works International Orange Edition.

in the form of black side stripes, a Midnight Black metallic spoiler, carbon fibre mirror caps, and a black fuel filler cap and door handles. The wheels were 18-inch Double Spoke John Cooper Works Wheels with a Ferric Grey finish, and there were chrome tailpipe trims and decals on both front and rear bumpers. The JCW Pro Exhaust with its Bluetooth-controlled flap was also standard.

The later introduction was the more snappily titled JCW Knights Edition, which was announced in November 2018 at the Los Angeles International Auto Show and went on sale in the first quarter of 2019. This, too, was a three-door Hatch with the controllable exhaust flap in its specification. It came in Midnight Black with a Melting Silver roof, U-shaped bonnet stripe and mirror caps, and with Melting Silver side stripes framed in red. There were Piano Black trims, door handles and fuel filler cap, and chromed exhaust tips.

The MINI Challenge Race Series

The MINI Challenge race series was established in 2002 with support from BMW. Its purpose in the beginning was to provide a focus for motorsport activities dependent on the then-new MINI and to build a sporting heritage for the model that would eventually become separate from the sporting heritage of the original Mini.

The early series used Cooper models; a class for the Cooper S was added in 2004, and the 220 bhp JCW models gained their own class in 2010. In 2015, the first purpose-built F56 race cars appeared. Sadly, the series had to be drastically curtailed during the 2020 season as a result of the Covid-19 pandemic.

The 2015 MINI Challenge series in the UK saw brother and sister Charlie and Vicki Butler-Henderson driving identical JCW cars. These F56 types were the first models specially built for racing.

7

The Electric Mini

BMW was no stranger to electric power for cars by the time production of the MINI Electric began in January 2020. However, the brand's targets were characteristically ambitious, and just over a year later there was a public announcement that the electric MINI embodied the brand's future: there would be no further development of combustion-engined MINI models after 2025, and the brand would become all-electric from the early 2030s.

The first electric-powered BMW research car was built in 1972 and examples were displayed at the Olympic Games, which that year were held in the German brand's home town of Munich. The BMW 1602e was a brave attempt to create an electric version of a

BMW released several design sketches for the MINI Electric, partly at least to raise public perception that this was something new and exciting.

real car and was based on the then-current two-door BMW 1602 saloon. At the time, most attempts to build a battery-powered car were quirky little two-seaters, designed only for use on short commuting runs into cities, and the trend towards these was accelerated after the 1973 Oil Crisis. Like these, the 1602e was limited by the battery technology then available, which did not support a range of more than 20–30 miles on a single charge.

BMW continued to investigate battery propulsion as a future technology, and as an alternative also investigated hydrogen fuel-cell propulsion. Continuing to focus on realistic car designs rather than on city runabouts, the company came up with a most promising research model called the E1 in 1992, which was certainly intended only as a city runabout but did at least look like a real car. Unfortunately, battery technology was still not good enough, and one of the two prototypes was destroyed when its batteries caught fire.

By the start of the twenty-first century, the development of electric cars was being driven by the moral and political imperatives associated with climate change. In Britain, the government's Technology Strategy Board was responsible for oversight of work in the field, and in 2009 invited proposals for innovative, industry-led collaborative research projects involving ultra-low carbon vehicles. The aim of the Ultra Low Carbon Vehicle Demonstrator Programme was to encourage manufacturers to develop ultra-low carbon vehicles that customers would actually want to buy and bring them to market as rapidly as possible.

BMW, meanwhile, was planning a major field trial of battery-powered MINI test cars, and was planning a fleet of no fewer than 600 vehicles to be tested in multiple locations around the world. There were to be trials in Munich and Berlin, on the east and west coasts of the USA, in Beijing and Shenzen, and in Paris and Tokyo. The coincidence of timing

Some of the features in the design sketches were very much show car items, and did not reach the production models.

This MINI Electric Concept embodied several of the design features in those sketches, while previewing the Neon Yellow highlights that would be seen on the real thing.

with the British initiative was perfect, and on 24 June 2009 BMW announced that the British field trial would be linked to the government-sponsored programme, would last for twelve months and would evaluate the technical and social aspects of living with an all-electric vehicle in a real-world environment. It became one of eight similar projects in Britain supported by £25 million in funding from the Technology Strategy Board and the Department for Transport.

Such field trials were not entirely new, of course: there had been similar initiatives during the 1990s involving GM in the USA, and several German manufacturers as well. However, MINI were clearly confident that the technology was now mature enough to offer worthwhile results. (By this time, of course, Tesla in the USA were already demonstrating that electric cars were very much viable, even if they were expensive to buy.)

The British trial involved sixty-two members of the public and seventy-six pool users running a fleet of forty cars over two six-month periods between December 2009 and March 2011. The forty trials cars were simply known as MINI E models, and were two-seat derivatives of the existing MINI Hatch. The rear seats were lost to some of the battery-power technology. The battery was a state-of-the-art 35 kWh lithium-ion type that contained 5,088 individual cells, and drove a 204 bhp electric motor that generated 220Nm (162 lb ft) of torque. These were big outputs – arguably more than were really needed for a car typically powered by petrol or diesel engines of between about 90 bhp and about

140 bhp – but the figures were attention-grabbing, and they were also a demonstration of technological ability.

Consortium partner Scottish and Southern Energy provided special chargers so that the cars could be charged at the homes of the volunteers who participated in the trial. A full charge typically took 4.5 hours at 32 amps. The batteries were theoretically capable of providing a range of 149 miles, although BMW claimed that 112 miles was more realistic, and the MINI E was capable of a 95 mph top speed. The trial was run over 250,000 miles against a control group of conventional production cars that consisted of BMW 116i models and MINI Coopers.

The trial results were very interesting, and were announced in 2011. Users generally needed about a week to get used to the MINI E's unfamiliar characteristics such as charging, the range, the regenerative braking system and the low noise while running. The trials showed that the range available was wholly adequate for typical everyday use, as the UK average daily distance driven for private cars overall is less than 25 miles and the test cars typically covered a slightly higher mileage of 29.7 miles in a day. The drivers in the trial were impressed by the cars' fast pick-up and quick acceleration, and almost every one of them came away from the experiment saying that they would consider buying an

The real thing – almost. This is one of the MINI E models in the 2009 trials in Britain. From left to right, it is flanked by Lord Drayson (Minister for Science and Information), Andy Hear (General Manager of MINI UK), and Lord Adonis (Secretary of State for Transport).

The 2009–11 trials were run around the world and involved 600 cars. Although they were based on R56 second-generation Hatch models, these cars had only two seats.

electric car in the future. Some were particularly enthusiastic about the electric MINIs they had been driving.

After the trial, BMW gathered more valuable publicity for their work by arranging for the 40 MINI E models to be on the official fleet of cars for the 2012 Olympic Games in London. For good measure, these were supplemented by three-quarter-scale battery-powered Mini MINI models, painted in true blue paint with the 2012 Olympic logo and a white roof. These were used to shuttle track and field projectiles (such as javelins and discuses) back to competing athletes, and each one was powered by a 10 horsepower electric motor with a battery pack that gave thirty-five minutes of usage on a single charge.

However, a production battery-powered MINI was still some way off, and the immediate use of the research results was in the programme to produce the BMW i3, the first purpose-built electric vehicle to be manufactured by BMW, which was introduced in 2013. Bizarrely, in spite of the German company's earlier attempts to develop an electric car that looked entirely conventional, the i3 embodied a number of the quirky features that had been associated with the abortive electric city car runabouts in the 1960s and 1970s.

An electric MINI was most definitely still on the cards, however, and at the Frankfurt Show in September 2017 BMW displayed what was clearly a production-ready car as the MINI Electric Concept. Painted in Reflection Silver with Striking Yellow accents and highlights, the car had attention-grabbing lower side panels that would not be carried over to production, but in most other respects was a faithful reflection of what BMW had in mind. The Frankfurt display of course coincided with the introduction of the Plug-In Hybrid MINI Countryman (see Chapter 5) in a powerful demonstration that BMW was deadly serious about producing electric cars.

The Frankfurt 'tease' worked well, too. By mid-2019 BMW had gathered 15,000 expressions of interest from customers in a production version of the all-electric MINI. Against that background, the production car was announced on 9 July 2019 at the Oxford plant, and selected journalists were allowed a rather limited test drive on the Formula E (electric car racing) circuit in New York later that month. Manufacturing was to begin in late 2019 and the first deliveries were anticipated for spring 2020, with exports in the plan as well as sales in Britain.

BMW arranged a typically spectacular event to mark the launch of the MINI Electric at the end of January 2020. The European Commission had selected Lisbon in Portugal as the Green Capital of Europe 2020, and BMW selected Lisbon as the launch venue for its new model. The city had one of the world's densest networks of electric-vehicle charging points – more than 500 of them – and for the launch a powerful searchlight was connected

Really the real thing this time! This production car was pictured during the Lisbon light-up event, when EV charging points around the city were lit up at night by columns of light reaching into the sky. The MINI Electric had a Cooper-style bonnet to add appeal, although the air scoop was not functional.

Looking far less special than the Concept car, the MINI E nevertheless stood out thanks to its yellow highlights and badges. The UK registration plate is a dummy; this is actually a LHD car!

to each one of them and switched on at night. The pillars of light reaching into the night sky all over the city made the point very forcefully that there was no shortage of charging points for electric vehicles, as well as creating a spectacular visual event in their own right.

The original plan had been to call the electric MINI a Cooper SE, the Cooper S element suggesting similar power and performance to the car of that name while the E stood for Electric. But by the time manufacturing actually began, the name had been changed to the simpler, and probably less controversial, MINI Electric. At the Oxford plant, the new model was fully integrated into the production process, and came off the same assembly lines as the combustion-engined models. This allowed maximum production flexibility to meet global demand. As things would turn out, 2020 was a particularly difficult year and MINI assembly had to be suspended for the two months between 23 March and 18 May as a response to the coronavirus pandemic. Nevertheless, by the end of the year, a total of 17,580 MINI Electric models had been sold and delivered to customers around the world, 3,385 of which were in the UK.

The production car was a full four-seater, unlike the MINI E models of the 2009 test fleet, and the battery and powertrain were completely hidden so that the MINI Electric looked exactly like a standard three-door MINI Hatch. There were minor differences, of course, and most notably at the front end where there was a plain grey hexagonal panel instead of the familiar radiator grille, with a pair of yellow accent bars across it that distinguished this MINI from others. However, it was possible to have these bars deleted, along with the matching mirror bodies and special badging, if a customer so wished.

The lack of obvious differences from the MINI Hatch was undoubtedly one of the most impressive aspects of the MINI Electric. The body shell required almost no alteration, and the battery pack was cleverly fitted into a T-shape formed by the central tunnel and the space where combustion-engined models had the fuel tank. The 32.6 kWh battery pack did hang slightly below the original floor level, and so the ride height was raised by 15 mm (roughly 0.6 in) to compensate. This in turn called for slightly wider wheel arch extensions to restore the cosmetic balance, and also for a wheel choice limited to 16-inch or 17-inch sizes.

As for suspension, the new car used the standard MINI hardware but with reinforced lower front arms and with different spring and damper settings to suit the additional weight and its more rearward bias. That additional weight of around 130 kg put the MINI Electric up to around 1,350 kg (as compared to a minimum of 1,210 kg for the standard car), but that still made it one of the lightest electric vehicles then on sale.

Most of the powertrain was shared with the BMW i3, although there was also a fundamental difference in that the MINI used front-wheel drive while the i3 had rear-wheel drive. The electric motor fitted under the bonnet where an internal combustion engine normally went and promised 184 bhp and 199 lb ft of torque, rather less than on the 2009 test cars but enough to give the MINI Electric a top speed of 93 mph and a 0–62 mph acceleration time of 7.3 seconds. The battery could be charged to 80 per cent of its total 92Ah capacity in thirty-five minutes, and on a full charge gave a range of about 125 miles.

This range was not class-leading by any means, and the Peugeot e-208 boasted over 200 miles on a single charge. Nevertheless, it was enough. As Peter Schwarzenbauer, the BMW board member with responsibility for the MINI brand, pointed out, 'Nobody needs a big range in an urban car; it's psychological. An average drive for a MINI customer per day is 37 km (23 miles), so in theory, our customers can drive all week on a single charge.' BMW's line was that the battery chosen for production models gave the best compromise of price, range and handling.

Many contemporary electric cars had a self-consciously futuristic interior with excessive reliance on the currently fashionable touchscreens, but the MINI Electric presented its occupants with a dashboard barely changed from the standard type. The most obvious change was an elliptical screen behind the steering wheel in place of the standard rev counter, where information about speed and remaining battery charge was displayed. Instead of a gear lever, there was a lever to select one of the three power modes, and there was also a fashionable electronic handbrake instead of the conventional central lever.

When *Autocar* magazine tried one, they commented that 'the first impression you get from driving one is reassuringly familiar. Perhaps the biggest compliment you can pay MINI's first series production electric car is that it drives and handles exactly as you'd expect a MINI to, regardless of powertrain.' This and other reports also highlighted an interesting feature of the regenerative braking system that helped to maintain battery charge. On its highest setting, it created enough drag to slow the car down so that in town traffic it was possible to drive almost without using the brakes; the level of retardation dropped on the lower setting, but so, of course, did the level of recharging.

When the MINI Electric reached showrooms in March 2020, several countries including the UK had subsidy schemes in place to encourage the purchase of electric cars. As a result, in Britain, a MINI Electric could be had for less than a petrol-powered Cooper S with an otherwise equivalent specification. That made the car a considerable bargain, although it was one that could not last indefinitely. the electric MINI, however, was here to stay.

The Electric Pacesetter

Always keen to capitalise on publicity opportunities, BMW announced the MINI Electric Pacestter car on 30 March 2021.

This special vehicle was to be the new Safety Car for the ABB FIA Formula E World Championship race series, and to emphasise the motor sport connection it was 'inspired' by the John Cooper Works models and their racing heritage. The car was based on a MINI Electric and was created as a collaboration among MINI Design, BMW Motorsport, the FIA and the Formula E. It was, claimed the public relations website mini.co.uk, 'a design that seriously stands out. John Cooper Works chequered accents meet electric-inspired neon elements.'

Just within this book's cut-off date of twenty years since the MINI's introduction, the electric-power message was reinforced by the announcement of the MINI Electric Pacesetter Safety Car for the FIA's Formula E race series.